TEACHER'S PET PUBLICATIONS

PUZZLE PACK
for
Lord of the Flies

based on the book by
William Golding

Written by
William T. Collins

© 2005 Teacher's Pet Publications
All Rights Reserved

The materials in this packet are copyrighted
by Teacher's Pet Publications, Inc.

These pages may be duplicated by the purchaser
for use in the purchaser's own classroom.

Copying any of these materials and distributing them
for any other purpose is a violation of the copyright laws.

© 2005 Teacher's Pet Publications, Inc.
www.tpet.com

INTRODUCTION
If you already own the LitPlan for this title, this Puzzle Pack will refresh your Unit Resource Materials and Vocabulary Resource Materials sections plus give you additional materials you can substitute into the tests. If you do not already have a complete LitPlan, these pages will give you some supplemental materials to use with your own plan. There are two main groups of materials: one set for unit words (such as characters' names, symbols, places, etc.) and one set for vocabulary words associated with the book.

WORD LIST
There is a word list for both the unit words and the vocabulary words. These lists show you which words are being used in the materials and the clues or definitions being used for those words. You may want to give students a word list with clues/definitions to help them, or you may want students to only have a word list (without clues/definitions) if you want them to work a little harder. Both are available for duplication. The word lists can also be your "calling key" for the bingo games.

FILL IN THE BLANK AND MATCHING
There are 4 each of the fill in the blank and matching worksheets for both the unit and vocabulary words. These pages can be used either as extra worksheets for students or as objective parts of a unit test. They can be done individually if students need extra help or as a whole class activity to review the material covered.

MAGIC SQUARES
The magic squares not only reinforce the material covered but also work on reasoning and math skills. Many teachers have told us that their students really enjoy doing these!

WORD SEARCH PUZZLES
The word search words go in all directions, as indicated on your answer keys. Two of the word search puzzles have the clues listed rather than the words. This makes the puzzle a little more difficult, but it reinforces the material better. Two word search puzzles have words only for students who find the clue puzzles too difficult.

CROSSWORD PUZZLES
Both unit and vocabulary word sections have 4 crossword puzzles.

BINGO CARDS
There are 32 individual bingo cards for the unit words and 32 individual bingo cards for the vocabulary words. You can use your word list as a "call list," calling the words at random and marking them off of your list as you go, or you could use the flash cards by cutting them apart and drawing the words at random from a hat (or box or whatever). To make a better review, you might ask for the definition and spelling of each word as you call it out–or you could call out the definitions and have students tell you the words they need to look for on the puzzle.

JUGGLE LETTERS
The vocabulary juggle letter game is intended to help students learn the spellings of the words. One sheet has the definitions listed on it as an extra help for students who need it or to reinforce the definitions if you choose to do so.

FLASH CARDS
We've included a set of vocabulary flash cards you can duplicate, cut, and fold for your students. Some teachers make a few sets for general use by the class; others make a set for each student. Some teachers duplicate them for each student and have the students cut & fold their own. You can cut out just the words and put them in a hat, have each student pick out one word and write the definition and a sentence for that word. Students then swap words and papers, with the next student adding a sentence of his own under the last one. You can have students swap as many times as you like. Each time the student will read the sentences written prior to his own and then add a sentence. You can cut out the words and definitions separately and play "I Have; Who Has?" Each student in the room draws a word and definition. The first student says, "I have (the name of the word). Who has the definition?" The student with the definition reads it then says, "I have (the name of the vocabulary word she has). Who has the definition?" The round continues until all words and definitions have been given.

Lord of the Flies Word List

No.	Word	Clue/Definition
1.	ADULTS	There are no _____ on the island until the officer arrives
2.	AIRPLANE	Boys' transportation to the island
3.	BOULDER	It shatters the conch and Piggy
4.	CANDLE	Jack slashed the green _____ buds
5.	CASTLE	Maurice and Roger destroy the Littluns' sand _____
6.	CHIEF	Another name for leader
7.	CLIFF	Simon falls off one to the sands below
8.	CONCH	Shell, symbol of authority
9.	CONFLICT	Man vs. man, for example
10.	COOPERATION	Jack criticizes the boys for their lack of this
11.	CORPSE	Sam and Eric see the _____ of a parachutist
12.	CRY	Sob
13.	DANCE	The hunters' _____ was the act of killing
14.	DARKNESS	Symbolic of evil
15.	FACE	Jack paints his with clay
16.	FEAR	Feeling the Littluns had
17.	FIRE	Jack plans to steal it from Ralph and Piggy
18.	FLAT	Shape of the rock on which Piggy lands
19.	FOREST	Thickly wooded area
20.	GLASSES	The boys use Piggy's _____ to start the fire
21.	GOLDING	Author
22.	GOOD	_____ vs. evil
23.	GRIN	Expression on pig's face
24.	HESITATES	Jack does this when he lifts his knife to kill the piglet
25.	HIDE	Conceal
26.	HUNTERS	The choir boys become this; responsible for getting food
27.	JACK	Choir leader, ugly without silliness
28.	LITTLUNS	Name given to the numerous little children of the group
29.	LORD	_____ of the Flies
30.	MAURICE	Choir boy as big as Jack, grinning all the time
31.	MOUNTAIN	Place from which the boys see something like a great ape
32.	OFFICER	A British naval _____ saves Ralph
33.	PIGGY	Intelligent, reader and thinker rather than a boy of action
34.	PLAY	Jack announces to Ralph, I'm not going to _____ anymore. Not with you.
35.	RAIN	Water from the sky
36.	RALPH	Handsome, athletic, natural leader
37.	ROCK	Castle _____
38.	SAMNERIC	Sam and Eric; identical twins
39.	SAVAGE	An animal man
40.	SEA	The bodies of Simon and the parachutist are carried out to _____
41.	SIMON	Poetic, sensitive, loner, mysterious boy
42.	SKULL	Ralph encounters a grinning pig's _____
43.	SPEAR	Pointed stick
44.	STONES	Roger stalks Henry and throws these near him
45.	SUN	The boys used the _____'s rays to start a fire
46.	WOOD	It had to be collected to burn

Lord of the Flies Fill In The Blank 1

_____

1. Handsome, athletic, natural leader
2. An animal man
3. Poetic, sensitive, loner, mysterious boy
4. Boys' transportation to the island
5. A British naval _____ saves Ralph
6. Pointed stick
7. Another name for leader
8. Place from which the boys see something like a great ape
9. Choir boy as big as Jack, grinning all the time
10. Man vs. man, for example
11. Maurice and Roger destroy the Littluns' sand _____
12. Ralph encounters a grinning pig's _____
13. Author
14. It shatters the conch and Piggy
15. Conceal
16. There are no _____ on the island until the officer arrives
17. The choir boys become this; responsible for getting food
18. Intelligent, reader and thinker rather than a boy of action
19. Simon falls off one to the sands below
20. Shape of the rock on which Piggy lands

Lord of the Flies Fill In The Blank 1 Answer Key

Answer	Clue
RALPH	1. Handsome, athletic, natural leader
SAVAGE	2. An animal man
SIMON	3. Poetic, sensitive, loner, mysterious boy
AIRPLANE	4. Boys' transportation to the island
OFFICER	5. A British naval _____ saves Ralph
SPEAR	6. Pointed stick
CHIEF	7. Another name for leader
MOUNTAIN	8. Place from which the boys see something like a great ape
MAURICE	9. Choir boy as big as Jack, grinning all the time
CONFLICT	10. Man vs. man, for example
CASTLE	11. Maurice and Roger destroy the Littluns' sand _____
SKULL	12. Ralph encounters a grinning pig's _____
GOLDING	13. Author
BOULDER	14. It shatters the conch and Piggy
HIDE	15. Conceal
ADULTS	16. There are no _____ on the island until the officer arrives
HUNTERS	17. The choir boys become this; responsible for getting food
PIGGY	18. Intelligent, reader and thinker rather than a boy of action
CLIFF	19. Simon falls off one to the sands below
FLAT	20. Shape of the rock on which Piggy lands

Lord of the Flies Fill In The Blank 2

_____

1. Jack paints his with clay
2. Boys' transportation to the island
3. _____ vs. evil
4. Simon falls off one to the sands below
5. Shape of the rock on which Piggy lands
6. Jack does this when he lifts his knife to kill the piglet
7. Sam and Eric; identical twins
8. Symbolic of evil
9. Maurice and Roger destroy the Littluns' sand _____
10. Expression on pig's face
11. The hunters' _____ was the act of killing
12. Castle _____
13. It had to be collected to burn
14. Thickly wooded area
15. Poetic, sensitive, loner, mysterious boy
16. Jack slashed the green _____ buds
17. An animal man
18. Choir boy as big as Jack, grinning all the time
19. Man vs. man, for example
20. Sob

Lord of the Flies Fill In The Blank 2 Answer Key

FACE	1. Jack paints his with clay
AIRPLANE	2. Boys' transportation to the island
GOOD	3. _____ vs. evil
CLIFF	4. Simon falls off one to the sands below
FLAT	5. Shape of the rock on which Piggy lands
HESITATES	6. Jack does this when he lifts his knife to kill the piglet
SAMNERIC	7. Sam and Eric; identical twins
DARKNESS	8. Symbolic of evil
CASTLE	9. Maurice and Roger destroy the Littluns' sand _____
GRIN	10. Expression on pig's face
DANCE	11. The hunters' _____ was the act of killing
ROCK	12. Castle _____
WOOD	13. It had to be collected to burn
FOREST	14. Thickly wooded area
SIMON	15. Poetic, sensitive, loner, mysterious boy
CANDLE	16. Jack slashed the green _____ buds
SAVAGE	17. An animal man
MAURICE	18. Choir boy as big as Jack, grinning all the time
CONFLICT	19. Man vs. man, for example
CRY	20. Sob

Lord of the Flies Fill In The Blank 3

_____ 1. Shape of the rock on which Piggy lands

_____ 2. Shell, symbol of authority

_____ 3. Simon falls off one to the sands below

_____ 4. Man vs. man, for example

_____ 5. Choir leader, ugly without silliness

_____ 6. Boys' transportation to the island

_____ 7. _____ vs. evil

_____ 8. Author

_____ 9. The hunters' _____ was the act of killing

_____ 10. Jack slashed the green _____ buds

_____ 11. Water from the sky

_____ 12. Maurice and Roger destroy the Littluns' sand _____

_____ 13. It had to be collected to burn

_____ 14. Name given to the numerous little children of the group

_____ 15. Another name for leader

_____ 16. Choir boy as big as Jack, grinning all the time

_____ 17. Jack announces to Ralph, I'm not going to _____ anymore. Not with you.

_____ 18. Expression on pig's face

_____ 19. Castle _____

_____ 20. Thickly wooded area

Lord of the Flies Fill In The Blank 3 Answer Key

FLAT	1. Shape of the rock on which Piggy lands
CONCH	2. Shell, symbol of authority
CLIFF	3. Simon falls off one to the sands below
CONFLICT	4. Man vs. man, for example
JACK	5. Choir leader, ugly without silliness
AIRPLANE	6. Boys' transportation to the island
GOOD	7. _____ vs. evil
GOLDING	8. Author
DANCE	9. The hunters' _____ was the act of killing
CANDLE	10. Jack slashed the green _____ buds
RAIN	11. Water from the sky
CASTLE	12. Maurice and Roger destroy the Littluns' sand _____
WOOD	13. It had to be collected to burn
LITTLUNS	14. Name given to the numerous little children of the group
CHIEF	15. Another name for leader
MAURICE	16. Choir boy as big as Jack, grinning all the time
PLAY	17. Jack announces to Ralph, I'm not going to _____ anymore. Not with you.
GRIN	18. Expression on pig's face
ROCK	19. Castle _____
FOREST	20. Thickly wooded area

Lord of the Flies Fill In The Blank 4

_____ 1. Jack does this when he lifts his knife to kill the piglet

_____ 2. Simon falls off one to the sands below

_____ 3. The boys use Piggy's _____ to start the fire

_____ 4. There are no _____ on the island until the officer arrives

_____ 5. Sob

_____ 6. Sam and Eric; identical twins

_____ 7. _____ of the Flies

_____ 8. Author

_____ 9. Ralph encounters a grinning pig's _____

_____ 10. The bodies of Simon and the parachutist are carried out to _____

_____ 11. Expression on pig's face

_____ 12. Choir leader, ugly without silliness

_____ 13. Jack paints his with clay

_____ 14. Boys' transportation to the island

_____ 15. The choir boys become this; responsible for getting food

_____ 16. Poetic, sensitive, loner, mysterious boy

_____ 17. Man vs. man, for example

_____ 18. Jack plans to steal it from Ralph and Piggy

_____ 19. _____ vs. evil

_____ 20. Choir boy as big as Jack, grinning all the time

Lord of the Flies Fill In The Blank 4 Answer Key

HESITATES	1. Jack does this when he lifts his knife to kill the piglet
CLIFF	2. Simon falls off one to the sands below
GLASSES	3. The boys use Piggy's _____ to start the fire
ADULTS	4. There are no _____ on the island until the officer arrives
CRY	5. Sob
SAMNERIC	6. Sam and Eric; identical twins
LORD	7. _____ of the Flies
GOLDING	8. Author
SKULL	9. Ralph encounters a grinning pig's _____
SEA	10. The bodies of Simon and the parachutist are carried out to _____
GRIN	11. Expression on pig's face
JACK	12. Choir leader, ugly without silliness
FACE	13. Jack paints his with clay
AIRPLANE	14. Boys' transportation to the island
HUNTERS	15. The choir boys become this; responsible for getting food
SIMON	16. Poetic, sensitive, loner, mysterious boy
CONFLICT	17. Man vs. man, for example
FIRE	18. Jack plans to steal it from Ralph and Piggy
GOOD	19. _____ vs. evil
MAURICE	20. Choir boy as big as Jack, grinning all the time

Lord of the Flies Matching 1

___ 1. SKULL
___ 2. HESITATES
___ 3. LORD
___ 4. GRIN
___ 5. RALPH
___ 6. FLAT
___ 7. SEA
___ 8. MOUNTAIN
___ 9. WOOD
___ 10. FEAR
___ 11. STONES
___ 12. DARKNESS
___ 13. COOPERATION
___ 14. HIDE
___ 15. SAMNERIC
___ 16. CONCH
___ 17. MAURICE
___ 18. CLIFF
___ 19. CRY
___ 20. PLAY
___ 21. CASTLE
___ 22. DANCE
___ 23. SPEAR
___ 24. GLASSES
___ 25. SAVAGE

A. Expression on pig's face
B. Maurice and Roger destroy the Littluns' sand _____
C. Conceal
D. Choir boy as big as Jack, grinning all the time
E. Shape of the rock on which Piggy lands
F. Roger stalks Henry and throws these near him
G. Sob
H. The hunters' _____ was the act of killing
I. Sam and Eric; identical twins
J. The boys use Piggy's _____ to start the fire
K. Feeling the Littluns had
L. It had to be collected to burn
M. Jack criticizes the boys for their lack of this
N. Symbolic of evil
O. _____ of the Flies
P. Pointed stick
Q. Jack announces to Ralph, I'm not going to _____ anymore. Not with you.
R. Simon falls off one to the sands below
S. Ralph encounters a grinning pig's _____
T. Jack does this when he lifts his knife to kill the piglet
U. Shell, symbol of authority
V. The bodies of Simon and the parachutist are carried out to _____
W. Handsome, athletic, natural leader
X. An animal man
Y. Place from which the boys see something like a great ape

Lord of the Flies Matching 1 Answer Key

S - 1. SKULL	A. Expression on pig's face
T - 2. HESITATES	B. Maurice and Roger destroy the Littluns' sand _____
O - 3. LORD	C. Conceal
A - 4. GRIN	D. Choir boy as big as Jack, grinning all the time
W - 5. RALPH	E. Shape of the rock on which Piggy lands
E - 6. FLAT	F. Roger stalks Henry and throws these near him
V - 7. SEA	G. Sob
Y - 8. MOUNTAIN	H. The hunters' _____ was the act of killing
L - 9. WOOD	I. Sam and Eric; identical twins
K - 10. FEAR	J. The boys use Piggy's _____ to start the fire
F - 11. STONES	K. Feeling the Littluns had
N - 12. DARKNESS	L. It had to be collected to burn
M - 13. COOPERATION	M. Jack criticizes the boys for their lack of this
C - 14. HIDE	N. Symbolic of evil
I - 15. SAMNERIC	O. _____ of the Flies
U - 16. CONCH	P. Pointed stick
D - 17. MAURICE	Q. Jack announces to Ralph, I'm not going to _____ anymore. Not with you.
R - 18. CLIFF	R. Simon falls off one to the sands below
G - 19. CRY	S. Ralph encounters a grinning pig's _____
Q - 20. PLAY	T. Jack does this when he lifts his knife to kill the piglet
B - 21. CASTLE	U. Shell, symbol of authority
H - 22. DANCE	V. The bodies of Simon and the parachutist are carried out to _____
P - 23. SPEAR	W. Handsome, athletic, natural leader
J - 24. GLASSES	X. An animal man
X - 25. SAVAGE	Y. Place from which the boys see something like a great ape

Lord of the Flies Matching 2

___ 1. SEA
___ 2. CRY
___ 3. GOLDING
___ 4. CHIEF
___ 5. MOUNTAIN
___ 6. STONES
___ 7. GLASSES
___ 8. DANCE
___ 9. DARKNESS
___ 10. OFFICER
___ 11. CASTLE
___ 12. MAURICE
___ 13. AIRPLANE
___ 14. CANDLE
___ 15. GOOD
___ 16. BOULDER
___ 17. LITTLUNS
___ 18. PLAY
___ 19. SAMNERIC
___ 20. RALPH
___ 21. RAIN
___ 22. FOREST
___ 23. SKULL
___ 24. ROCK
___ 25. WOOD

A. Symbolic of evil
B. The hunters' _____ was the act of killing
C. Thickly wooded area
D. The boys use Piggy's _____ to start the fire
E. Ralph encounters a grinning pig's _____
F. A British naval _____ saves Ralph
G. It shatters the conch and Piggy
H. Author
I. Castle _____
J. Sob
K. Place from which the boys see something like a great ape
L. Boys' transportation to the island
M. Sam and Eric; identical twins
N. Another name for leader
O. It had to be collected to burn
P. Jack slashed the green _____ buds
Q. Water from the sky
R. Name given to the numerous little children of the group
S. Roger stalks Henry and throws these near him
T. The bodies of Simon and the parachutist are carried out to _____
U. Choir boy as big as Jack, grinning all the time
V. Jack announces to Ralph, I'm not going to _____ anymore. Not with you.
W. Handsome, athletic, natural leader
X. Maurice and Roger destroy the Littluns' sand _____
Y. _____ vs. evil

Lord of the Flies Matching 2 Answer Key

- T - 1. SEA
- J - 2. CRY
- H - 3. GOLDING
- N - 4. CHIEF
- K - 5. MOUNTAIN
- S - 6. STONES
- D - 7. GLASSES
- B - 8. DANCE
- A - 9. DARKNESS
- F - 10. OFFICER
- X - 11. CASTLE
- U - 12. MAURICE
- L - 13. AIRPLANE
- P - 14. CANDLE
- Y - 15. GOOD
- G - 16. BOULDER
- R - 17. LITTLUNS
- V - 18. PLAY
- M - 19. SAMNERIC
- W - 20. RALPH
- Q - 21. RAIN
- C - 22. FOREST
- E - 23. SKULL
- I - 24. ROCK
- O - 25. WOOD

A. Symbolic of evil
B. The hunters' _____ was the act of killing
C. Thickly wooded area
D. The boys use Piggy's _____ to start the fire
E. Ralph encounters a grinning pig's _____
F. A British naval _____ saves Ralph
G. It shatters the conch and Piggy
H. Author
I. Castle _____
J. Sob
K. Place from which the boys see something like a great ape
L. Boys' transportation to the island
M. Sam and Eric; identical twins
N. Another name for leader
O. It had to be collected to burn
P. Jack slashed the green _____ buds
Q. Water from the sky
R. Name given to the numerous little children of the group
S. Roger stalks Henry and throws these near him
T. The bodies of Simon and the parachutist are carried out to _____
U. Choir boy as big as Jack, grinning all the time
V. Jack announces to Ralph, I'm not going to _____ anymore. Not with you.
W. Handsome, athletic, natural leader
X. Maurice and Roger destroy the Littluns' sand _____
Y. _____ vs. evil

Lord of the Flies Matching 3

___ 1. SUN
___ 2. CONCH
___ 3. ADULTS
___ 4. FOREST
___ 5. OFFICER
___ 6. CORPSE
___ 7. LORD
___ 8. GRIN
___ 9. SPEAR
___ 10. SIMON
___ 11. ROCK
___ 12. PIGGY
___ 13. RALPH
___ 14. HUNTERS
___ 15. AIRPLANE
___ 16. DANCE
___ 17. BOULDER
___ 18. SKULL
___ 19. HESITATES
___ 20. SEA
___ 21. CHIEF
___ 22. COOPERATION
___ 23. MOUNTAIN
___ 24. HIDE
___ 25. CONFLICT

A. There are no _____ on the island until the officer arrives
B. Castle _____
C. Man vs. man, for example
D. The hunters' _____ was the act of killing
E. Ralph encounters a grinning pig's _____
F. Expression on pig's face
G. Pointed stick
H. The choir boys become this; responsible for getting food
I. Place from which the boys see something like a great ape
J. Jack does this when he lifts his knife to kill the piglet
K. Sam and Eric see the _____ of a parachutist
L. Poetic, sensitive, loner, mysterious boy
M. Thickly wooded area
N. Shell, symbol of authority
O. Another name for leader
P. _____ of the Flies
Q. Handsome, athletic, natural leader
R. Intelligent, reader and thinker rather than a boy of action
S. Conceal
T. The boys used the _____'s rays to start a fire
U. Jack criticizes the boys for their lack of this
V. Boys' transportation to the island
W. A British naval _____ saves Ralph
X. It shatters the conch and Piggy
Y. The bodies of Simon and the parachutist are carried out to _____

Lord of the Flies Matching 3 Answer Key

T - 1. SUN	A. There are no _____ on the island until the officer arrives
N - 2. CONCH	B. Castle _____
A - 3. ADULTS	C. Man vs. man, for example
M - 4. FOREST	D. The hunters' _____ was the act of killing
W - 5. OFFICER	E. Ralph encounters a grinning pig's _____
K - 6. CORPSE	F. Expression on pig's face
P - 7. LORD	G. Pointed stick
F - 8. GRIN	H. The choir boys become this; responsible for getting food
G - 9. SPEAR	I. Place from which the boys see something like a great ape
L - 10. SIMON	J. Jack does this when he lifts his knife to kill the piglet
B - 11. ROCK	K. Sam and Eric see the _____ of a parachutist
R - 12. PIGGY	L. Poetic, sensitive, loner, mysterious boy
Q - 13. RALPH	M. Thickly wooded area
H - 14. HUNTERS	N. Shell, symbol of authority
V - 15. AIRPLANE	O. Another name for leader
D - 16. DANCE	P. _____ of the Flies
X - 17. BOULDER	Q. Handsome, athletic, natural leader
E - 18. SKULL	R. Intelligent, reader and thinker rather than a boy of action
J - 19. HESITATES	S. Conceal
Y - 20. SEA	T. The boys used the _____'s rays to start a fire
O - 21. CHIEF	U. Jack criticizes the boys for their lack of this
U - 22. COOPERATION	V. Boys' transportation to the island
I - 23. MOUNTAIN	W. A British naval _____ saves Ralph
S - 24. HIDE	X. It shatters the conch and Piggy
C - 25. CONFLICT	Y. The bodies of Simon and the parachutist are carried out to _____

Lord of the Flies Matching 4

___ 1. LITTLUNS
___ 2. RAIN
___ 3. SAMNERIC
___ 4. CHIEF
___ 5. FIRE
___ 6. CONCH
___ 7. CASTLE
___ 8. JACK
___ 9. DANCE
___ 10. SKULL
___ 11. STONES
___ 12. SEA
___ 13. CONFLICT
___ 14. MAURICE
___ 15. GOLDING
___ 16. HUNTERS
___ 17. DARKNESS
___ 18. MOUNTAIN
___ 19. GOOD
___ 20. CLIFF
___ 21. CRY
___ 22. FACE
___ 23. ROCK
___ 24. SAVAGE
___ 25. GRIN

A. The hunters' _____ was the act of killing
B. Symbolic of evil
C. Castle _____
D. Simon falls off one to the sands below
E. Shell, symbol of authority
F. Expression on pig's face
G. Sam and Eric; identical twins
H. Maurice and Roger destroy the Littluns' sand _____
I. Choir boy as big as Jack, grinning all the time
J. Sob
K. Jack plans to steal it from Ralph and Piggy
L. Man vs. man, for example
M. Ralph encounters a grinning pig's _____
N. The bodies of Simon and the parachutist are carried out to _____
O. Water from the sky
P. Choir leader, ugly without silliness
Q. Name given to the numerous little children of the group
R. Jack paints his with clay
S. The choir boys become this; responsible for getting food
T. An animal man
U. Another name for leader
V. Roger stalks Henry and throws these near him
W. Place from which the boys see something like a great ape
X. _____ vs. evil
Y. Author

Lord of the Flies Matching 4 Answer Key

Q - 1. LITTLUNS
O - 2. RAIN
G - 3. SAMNERIC
U - 4. CHIEF
K - 5. FIRE
E - 6. CONCH
H - 7. CASTLE
P - 8. JACK
A - 9. DANCE
M - 10. SKULL
V - 11. STONES
N - 12. SEA
L - 13. CONFLICT
I - 14. MAURICE
Y - 15. GOLDING
S - 16. HUNTERS
B - 17. DARKNESS
W - 18. MOUNTAIN
X - 19. GOOD
D - 20. CLIFF
J - 21. CRY
R - 22. FACE
C - 23. ROCK
T - 24. SAVAGE
F - 25. GRIN

A. The hunters' _____ was the act of killing
B. Symbolic of evil
C. Castle _____
D. Simon falls off one to the sands below
E. Shell, symbol of authority
F. Expression on pig's face
G. Sam and Eric; identical twins
H. Maurice and Roger destroy the Littluns' sand _____
I. Choir boy as big as Jack, grinning all the time
J. Sob
K. Jack plans to steal it from Ralph and Piggy
L. Man vs. man, for example
M. Ralph encounters a grinning pig's _____
N. The bodies of Simon and the parachutist are carried out to _____
O. Water from the sky
P. Choir leader, ugly without silliness
Q. Name given to the numerous little children of the group
R. Jack paints his with clay
S. The choir boys become this; responsible for getting food
T. An animal man
U. Another name for leader
V. Roger stalks Henry and throws these near him
W. Place from which the boys see something like a great ape
X. _____ vs. evil
Y. Author

Lord of the Flies Magic Squares 1

Match the definition with the vocabulary word. Put your answers in the magic squares below. When your answers are correct, all columns and rows will add to the same number.

A. OFFICER
B. CRY
C. WOOD
D. FACE
E. RAIN
F. COOPERATION
G. CONFLICT
H. MAURICE
I. SAMNERIC
J. LITTLUNS
K. ROCK
L. SUN
M. FOREST
N. BOULDER
O. FLAT
P. CHIEF

1. Jack criticizes the boys for their lack of this
2. Sam and Eric; identical twins
3. Shape of the rock on which Piggy lands
4. Jack paints his with clay
5. Thickly wooded area
6. Sob
7. Choir boy as big as Jack, grinning all the time
8. Castle _____
9. It had to be collected to burn
10. Another name for leader
11. Name given to the numerous little children of the group
12. Water from the sky
13. The boys used the _____'s rays to start a fire
14. Man vs. man, for example
15. A British naval _____ saves Ralph
16. It shatters the conch and Piggy

A=	B=	C=	D=
E=	F=	G=	H=
I=	J=	K=	L=
M=	N=	O=	P=

Lord of the Flies Magic Squares 1 Answer Key

Match the definition with the vocabulary word. Put your answers in the magic squares below. When your answers are correct, all columns and rows will add to the same number.

A. OFFICER
B. CRY
C. WOOD
D. FACE
E. RAIN
F. COOPERATION
G. CONFLICT
H. MAURICE
I. SAMNERIC
J. LITTLUNS
K. ROCK
L. SUN
M. FOREST
N. BOULDER
O. FLAT
P. CHIEF

1. Jack criticizes the boys for their lack of this
2. Sam and Eric; identical twins
3. Shape of the rock on which Piggy lands
4. Jack paints his with clay
5. Thickly wooded area
6. Sob
7. Choir boy as big as Jack, grinning all the time
8. Castle _____
9. It had to be collected to burn
10. Another name for leader
11. Name given to the numerous little children of the group
12. Water from the sky
13. The boys used the _____'s rays to start a fire
14. Man vs. man, for example
15. A British naval _____ saves Ralph
16. It shatters the conch and Piggy

A=15	B=6	C=9	D=4
E=12	F=1	G=14	H=7
I=2	J=11	K=8	L=13
M=5	N=16	O=3	P=10

Lord of the Flies Magic Squares 2

Match the definition with the vocabulary word. Put your answers in the magic squares below. When your answers are correct, all columns and rows will add to the same number.

A. ADULTS
B. CRY
C. FOREST
D. FACE
E. RALPH
F. ROCK
G. WOOD
H. GOOD
I. OFFICER
J. LITTLUNS
K. MOUNTAIN
L. DANCE
M. SAVAGE
N. RAIN
O. PIGGY
P. AIRPLANE

1. _____ vs. evil
2. An animal man
3. Sob
4. Place from which the boys see something like a great ape
5. Name given to the numerous little children of the group
6. Thickly wooded area
7. Boys' transportation to the island
8. Handsome, athletic, natural leader
9. Intelligent, reader and thinker rather than a boy of action
10. Castle _____
11. A British naval _____ saves Ralph
12. Jack paints his with clay
13. There are no _____ on the island until the officer arrives
14. The hunters' _____ was the act of killing
15. It had to be collected to burn
16. Water from the sky

A=	B=	C=	D=
E=	F=	G=	H=
I=	J=	K=	L=
M=	N=	O=	P=

23
Copyrighted

Lord of the Flies Magic Squares 2 Answer Key

Match the definition with the vocabulary word. Put your answers in the magic squares below. When your answers are correct, all columns and rows will add to the same number.

A. ADULTS
B. CRY
C. FOREST
D. FACE
E. RALPH
F. ROCK
G. WOOD
H. GOOD
I. OFFICER
J. LITTLUNS
K. MOUNTAIN
L. DANCE
M. SAVAGE
N. RAIN
O. PIGGY
P. AIRPLANE

1. _____ vs. evil
2. An animal man
3. Sob
4. Place from which the boys see something like a great ape
5. Name given to the numerous little children of the group
6. Thickly wooded area
7. Boys' transportation to the island
8. Handsome, athletic, natural leader
9. Intelligent, reader and thinker rather than a boy of action
10. Castle _____
11. A British naval _____ saves Ralph
12. Jack paints his with clay
13. There are no _____ on the island until the officer arrives
14. The hunters' _____ was the act of killing
15. It had to be collected to burn
16. Water from the sky

A=13	B=3	C=6	D=12
E=8	F=10	G=15	H=1
I=11	J=5	K=4	L=14
M=2	N=16	O=9	P=7

Lord of the Flies Magic Squares 3

Match the definition with the vocabulary word. Put your answers in the magic squares below. When your answers are correct, all columns and rows will add to the same number.

A. WOOD
B. SKULL
C. CHIEF
D. RAIN
E. OFFICER
F. STONES
G. HESITATES
H. CRY
I. FEAR
J. GRIN
K. JACK
L. HIDE
M. GOOD
N. RALPH
O. SUN
P. MOUNTAIN

1. It had to be collected to burn
2. Handsome, athletic, natural leader
3. Expression on pig's face
4. A British naval _____ saves Ralph
5. Jack does this when he lifts his knife to kill the piglet
6. Conceal
7. Place from which the boys see something like a great ape
8. Another name for leader
9. The boys used the _____'s rays to start a fire
10. Water from the sky
11. Sob
12. Choir leader, ugly without silliness
13. Feeling the Littluns had
14. Roger stalks Henry and throws these near him
15. Ralph encounters a grinning pig's _____
16. _____ vs. evil

A=	B=	C=	D=
E=	F=	G=	H=
I=	J=	K=	L=
M=	N=	O=	P=

Lord of the Flies Magic Squares 3 Answer Key

Match the definition with the vocabulary word. Put your answers in the magic squares below. When your answers are correct, all columns and rows will add to the same number.

A. WOOD
B. SKULL
C. CHIEF
D. RAIN
E. OFFICER
F. STONES
G. HESITATES
H. CRY
I. FEAR
J. GRIN
K. JACK
L. HIDE
M. GOOD
N. RALPH
O. SUN
P. MOUNTAIN

1. It had to be collected to burn
2. Handsome, athletic, natural leader
3. Expression on pig's face
4. A British naval _____ saves Ralph
5. Jack does this when he lifts his knife to kill the piglet
6. Conceal
7. Place from which the boys see something like a great ape
8. Another name for leader
9. The boys used the _____'s rays to start a fire
10. Water from the sky
11. Sob
12. Choir leader, ugly without silliness
13. Feeling the Littluns had
14. Roger stalks Henry and throws these near him
15. Ralph encounters a grinning pig's _____
16. _____ vs. evil

A=1	B=15	C=8	D=10
E=4	F=14	G=5	H=11
I=13	J=3	K=12	L=6
M=16	N=2	O=9	P=7

Lord of the Flies Magic Squares 4

Match the definition with the vocabulary word. Put your answers in the magic squares below. When your answers are correct, all columns and rows will add to the same number.

A. CONCH
B. FOREST
C. SKULL
D. SPEAR
E. LITTLUNS
F. FLAT
G. SIMON
H. FACE
I. CRY
J. SUN
K. PLAY
L. RAIN
M. WOOD
N. HUNTERS
O. MOUNTAIN
P. DANCE

1. It had to be collected to burn
2. Shape of the rock on which Piggy lands
3. Jack paints his with clay
4. Place from which the boys see something like a great ape
5. Water from the sky
6. Ralph encounters a grinning pig's _____
7. Shell, symbol of authority
8. The boys used the _____'s rays to start a fire
9. Jack announces to Ralph, I'm not going to _____ anymore. Not with you.
10. Pointed stick
11. Thickly wooded area
12. Sob
13. The choir boys become this; responsible for getting food
14. Name given to the numerous little children of the group
15. Poetic, sensitive, loner, mysterious boy
16. The hunters' _____ was the act of killing

A=	B=	C=	D=
E=	F=	G=	H=
I=	J=	K=	L=
M=	N=	O=	P=

Lord of the Flies Magic Squares 4 Answer Key

Match the definition with the vocabulary word. Put your answers in the magic squares below. When your answers are correct, all columns and rows will add to the same number.

A. CONCH
B. FOREST
C. SKULL
D. SPEAR
E. LITTLUNS
F. FLAT

G. SIMON
H. FACE
I. CRY
J. SUN
K. PLAY
L. RAIN

M. WOOD
N. HUNTERS
O. MOUNTAIN
P. DANCE

1. It had to be collected to burn
2. Shape of the rock on which Piggy lands
3. Jack paints his with clay
4. Place from which the boys see something like a great ape
5. Water from the sky
6. Ralph encounters a grinning pig's _____
7. Shell, symbol of authority
8. The boys used the _____'s rays to start a fire
9. Jack announces to Ralph, I'm not going to _____ anymore. Not with you.
10. Pointed stick
11. Thickly wooded area
12. Sob
13. The choir boys become this; responsible for getting food
14. Name given to the numerous little children of the group
15. Poetic, sensitive, loner, mysterious boy
16. The hunters' _____ was the act of killing

A=7	B=11	C=6	D=10
E=14	F=2	G=15	H=3
I=12	J=8	K=9	L=5
M=1	N=13	O=4	P=16

Lord of the Flies Word Search 1

```
M O U N T A I N P M A U R I C E G S
C O R P S E R J R E C I F F O J T Y
B E X N S C F E C P P F X O F O F J
K C R P K T L L G H F A X R N Y P L
D N E N B A M D C J I C C E B V P E
T A I R P L A N E N S E S S A L G R
R D R I Z F O A Z O D L F T A A H G
T C G K Z C J C S I M O N Y V D D C
H G O B N T L V H T F M L A C H Y S
Y H U N T E R S H A N U S R A I N X
S E W F F D S P G R B A K S S F Z Q
A S N O Q L L S N E O D U T T I Q R
M I Q R O A I B D P U U L B L R P P
N T L O R D K C Y O L L L C E E N Y
E A D W O C N R T O D T J V L I G R
R T Z O O X C R C C E S A W R I M G
I E G R S E A F E A R P C G S S F Q
C S N U L T T I L H B K K G T W W F
```

A British naval _____ saves Ralph (7)
An animal man (6)
Another name for leader (5)
Boys' transportation to the island (8)
Castle _____ (4)
Choir boy as big as Jack, grinning all the time (7)
Choir leader, ugly without silliness (4)
Conceal (4)
Expression on pig's face (4)
Feeling the Littluns had (4)
Handsome, athletic, natural leader (5)
Intelligent, reader and thinker rather than a boy of action (5)
It had to be collected to burn (4)
It shatters the conch and Piggy (7)
Jack announces to Ralph, I'm not going to _____ anymore. Not with you. (4)
Jack criticizes the boys for their lack of this (11)
Jack does this when he lifts his knife to kill the piglet (9)
Jack paints his with clay (4)
Jack plans to steal it from Ralph and Piggy (4)
Jack slashed the green _____ buds (6)
Man vs. man, for example (8)
Maurice and Roger destroy the Littluns' sand _____ (6)
Name given to the numerous little children of the group (8)
Place from which the boys see something like a great ape (8)
Poetic, sensitive, loner, mysterious boy (5)
Pointed stick (5)
Ralph encounters a grinning pig's _____ (5)
Roger stalks Henry and throws these near him (6)
Sam and Eric see the _____ of a parachutist (6)
Sam and Eric; identical twins (8)
Shape of the rock on which Piggy lands (4)
Shell, symbol of authority (5)
Simon falls off one to the sands below (5)
Sob (3)
Symbolic of evil (8)
The bodies of Simon and the parachutist are carried out to _____ (3)
The boys use Piggy's _____ to start the fire (7)
The boys used the _____'s rays to start a fire (3)
The choir boys become this; responsible for getting food (7)
The hunters' _____ was the act of killing (5)
There are no _____ on the island until the officer arrives (6)
Thickly wooded area (6)
Water from the sky (4)
_____ of the Flies (4)
_____ vs. evil (4)

Lord of the Flies Word Search 1 Answer Key

```
M O U N T A I N     M A U R I C E   S
C O R P S E     R E C I F F O   T
    E   S     E   C     F   O   O
    C   P   T   L   H   A   R   N
D N E   A   D C   I   C   E     P E
  A R P L A N E N S E S S A L G
R D R   F O   A   C   F T A A
  C G K   C   C S I M O N Y V
  G O   N       H T     A C
Y H U N T E R S H A N U S R A I N
S E W   F   S P   R B A   S F
A S   O   L L S   E O D   T I
M I     O A I     P U L   L R
N T   L O R D K C Y O L L C E E N
E A     O C   R T O D T J   L I
R T     O O   C   C E S A   R
I E   G R S E A F E A R   C G   F
C S   N U L T T I L       K       F
```

A British naval _____ saves Ralph (7)
An animal man (6)
Another name for leader (5)
Boys' transportation to the island (8)
Castle _____ (4)
Choir boy as big as Jack, grinning all the time (7)
Choir leader, ugly without silliness (4)
Conceal (4)
Expression on pig's face (4)
Feeling the Littluns had (4)
Handsome, athletic, natural leader (5)
Intelligent, reader and thinker rather than a boy of action (5)
It had to be collected to burn (4)
It shatters the conch and Piggy (7)
Jack announces to Ralph, I'm not going to _____ anymore. Not with you. (4)
Jack criticizes the boys for their lack of this (11)
Jack does this when he lifts his knife to kill the piglet (9)
Jack paints his with clay (4)
Jack plans to steal it from Ralph and Piggy (4)
Jack slashed the green _____ buds (6)
Man vs. man, for example (8)
Maurice and Roger destroy the Littluns' sand _____ (6)
Name given to the numerous little children of the group (8)
Place from which the boys see something like a great ape (8)
Poetic, sensitive, loner, mysterious boy (5)
Pointed stick (5)
Ralph encounters a grinning pig's _____ (5)
Roger stalks Henry and throws these near him (6)
Sam and Eric see the _____ of a parachutist (6)
Sam and Eric; identical twins (8)
Shape of the rock on which Piggy lands (4)
Shell, symbol of authority (5)
Simon falls off one to the sands below (5)
Sob (3)
Symbolic of evil (8)
The bodies of Simon and the parachutist are carried out to _____ (3)
The boys use Piggy's _____ to start the fire (7)
The boys used the _____'s rays to start a fire (3)
The choir boys become this; responsible for getting food (7)
The hunters' _____ was the act of killing (5)
There are no _____ on the island until the officer arrives (6)
Thickly wooded area (6)
Water from the sky (4)
_____ of the Flies (4)
_____ vs. evil (4)

Lord of the Flies Word Search 2

```
X Q H Q Q G G F O R E S T S M F R H
N S H N L N R S S M L N C G O A C B
B Y T Q I S S I C K K F Q O U C B P
L O R D T E D A N C E S T O N E S V
F T L A S A O D O A S K U D T C C X
W O L S D L O R J P U R N A I H Z
G F A T P E W E H S R L A D I R I W
F L P I G L L D A P O L L A N U E N
G V D A R D A M W E C H P R H A F K
T Q V N N P N Y N A L I H K E M H Y
J A I A C E L O T R I D T N S P U Y
S A C R R A M A Q W F E Y E I H N L
R R C I R I S S N L F G R S T F T H
N P C Z S N L T B E G Z C S A C E Q
S N U L T T I L L I H Z M M T V R V
G K J W D V S U P E R I F Q E D S Z
D Z X K N H H D G C R Y V N S X Z V
B O U L D E R A X O F F I C E R W M
```

A British naval _____ saves Ralph (7)
An animal man (6)
Another name for leader (5)
Author (7)
Boys' transportation to the island (8)
Castle _____ (4)
Choir boy as big as Jack, grinning all the time (7)
Choir leader, ugly without silliness (4)
Conceal (4)
Expression on pig's face (4)
Feeling the Littluns had (4)
Handsome, athletic, natural leader (5)
Intelligent, reader and thinker rather than a boy of action (5)
It had to be collected to burn (4)
It shatters the conch and Piggy (7)
Jack announces to Ralph, I'm not going to _____ anymore. Not with you. (4)
Jack does this when he lifts his knife to kill the piglet (9)
Jack paints his with clay (4)
Jack plans to steal it from Ralph and Piggy (4)
Jack slashed the green _____ buds (6)
Maurice and Roger destroy the Littluns' sand _____ (6)
Name given to the numerous little children of the group (8)
Place from which the boys see something like a great ape (8)

Poetic, sensitive, loner, mysterious boy (5)
Pointed stick (5)
Ralph encounters a grinning pig's _____ (5)
Roger stalks Henry and throws these near him (6)
Sam and Eric see the _____ of a parachutist (6)
Sam and Eric; identical twins (8)
Shape of the rock on which Piggy lands (4)
Shell, symbol of authority (5)
Simon falls off one to the sands below (5)
Sob (3)
Symbolic of evil (8)
The bodies of Simon and the parachutist are carried out to _____ (3)
The boys use Piggy's _____ to start the fire (7)
The boys used the _____'s rays to start a fire (3)
The choir boys become this; responsible for getting food (7)
The hunters' _____ was the act of killing (5)
There are no _____ on the island until the officer arrives (6)
Thickly wooded area (6)
Water from the sky (4)
_____ of the Flies (4)
_____ vs. evil (4)

Lord of the Flies Word Search 2 Answer Key

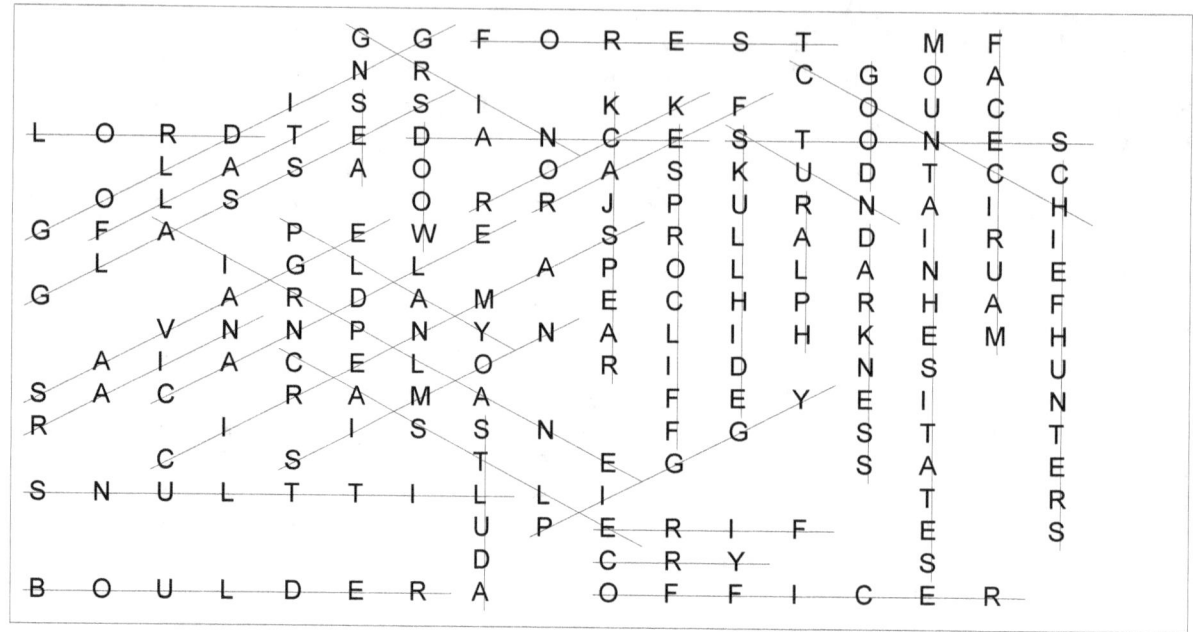

A British naval _____ saves Ralph (7)
An animal man (6)
Another name for leader (5)
Author (7)
Boys' transportation to the island (8)
Castle _____ (4)
Choir boy as big as Jack, grinning all the time (7)
Choir leader, ugly without silliness (4)
Conceal (4)
Expression on pig's face (4)
Feeling the Littluns had (4)
Handsome, athletic, natural leader (5)
Intelligent, reader and thinker rather than a boy of action (5)
It had to be collected to burn (4)
It shatters the conch and Piggy (7)
Jack announces to Ralph, I'm not going to _____ anymore. Not with you. (4)
Jack does this when he lifts his knife to kill the piglet (9)
Jack paints his with clay (4)
Jack plans to steal it from Ralph and Piggy (4)
Jack slashed the green _____ buds (6)
Maurice and Roger destroy the Littluns' sand _____ (6)
Name given to the numerous little children of the group (8)
Place from which the boys see something like a great ape (8)

Poetic, sensitive, loner, mysterious boy (5)
Pointed stick (5)
Ralph encounters a grinning pig's _____ (5)
Roger stalks Henry and throws these near him (6)
Sam and Eric see the _____ of a parachutist (6)
Sam and Eric; identical twins (8)
Shape of the rock on which Piggy lands (4)
Shell, symbol of authority (5)
Simon falls off one to the sands below (5)
Sob (3)
Symbolic of evil (8)
The bodies of Simon and the parachutist are carried out to _____ (3)
The boys use Piggy's _____ to start the fire (7)
The boys used the _____'s rays to start a fire (3)
The choir boys become this; responsible for getting food (7)
The hunters' _____ was the act of killing (5)
There are no _____ on the island until the officer arrives (6)
Thickly wooded area (6)
Water from the sky (4)
_____ of the Flies (4)
_____ vs. evil (4)

Lord of the Flies Word Search 3

```
N M A U R I C E M Q H G O L D I N G
Q L O J P O K T F Q Z O S H H P F Q
A I H U N R E C I F F O S T S E S P
D T Q C N F J G F V B D M S I W W N
U T H C D T H L J O K S T H H M O N
L L D K R Y A I K R R O C S Z I C K
T U H C S P F I D A N E R E T M L N
S N A I R P L A N E L T S A C P I X
P S M R S T A A S F K R R T I R F K
H O J E C D T P Y S E E O G G N F G
N V N N Z P R P E T P D G C G X D N
J U Z M R O R S N O A Y R R K R F P
S K V A C J S U O R V E Y Y O Z H D
T X R S Y A H C K P D D D L R P X D
S K U L L C O N F L I C T A L F D P
Y S Y G S K E X U A L Y E A N O H J
E G A V A S S O Q L C P R J O C P B
F I R E S V B Z S L S E L W D Y E D
```

ADULTS	DANCE	HIDE	RALPH
AIRPLANE	DARKNESS	HUNTERS	ROCK
BOULDER	FACE	JACK	SAMNERIC
CASTLE	FEAR	LITTLUNS	SAVAGE
CHIEF	FIRE	LORD	SEA
CLIFF	FLAT	MAURICE	SIMON
CONCH	FOREST	MOUNTAIN	SKULL
CONFLICT	GLASSES	OFFICER	SPEAR
COOPERATION	GOLDING	PIGGY	STONES
CORPSE	GOOD	PLAY	SUN
CRY	GRIN	RAIN	WOOD

Lord of the Flies Word Search 3 Answer Key

ADULTS	DANCE	HIDE	RALPH
AIRPLANE	DARKNESS	HUNTERS	ROCK
BOULDER	FACE	JACK	SAMNERIC
CASTLE	FEAR	LITTLUNS	SAVAGE
CHIEF	FIRE	LORD	SEA
CLIFF	FLAT	MAURICE	SIMON
CONCH	FOREST	MOUNTAIN	SKULL
CONFLICT	GLASSES	OFFICER	SPEAR
COOPERATION	GOLDING	PIGGY	STONES
CORPSE	GOOD	PLAY	SUN
CRY	GRIN	RAIN	WOOD

Lord of the Flies Word Search 4

```
F E A R G F P D M O U N T A I N F F
E H D C L L G A C M R N X K H F K Y
I E U D A A O N O N A R M B I P F R
H S L Y S T C O N I X C L D W Z X
C I T B S G D E F I Y C O F A C E
T T S G E N V F L T F R O G N K D Q
H A N J S I H H I A B W Y H R C Y Q
U T N E K D P X C R B F R E Q E H B
N E S C S L F P T E O R N N Y L C D
T S K I A O E I Z P U N V A L T W H
E H G R S G L G F O L F W L D S D T
R L J U Z U D G I O D R O P D A B L
S A V A G E N Y R C E S P R O C K Z
C P E M C X A N E C R K O I E P Z K
T S E F R K C G I R F L P A Y S T Y
J K D A K Z S F D A R K N E S S T T
G R I N R Y F S T O N E S I M O N M
C B H J N O L I T T L U N S K U L L
```

ADULTS	DANCE	HIDE	ROCK
AIRPLANE	DARKNESS	HUNTERS	SAVAGE
BOULDER	FACE	JACK	SEA
CANDLE	FEAR	LITTLUNS	SIMON
CASTLE	FIRE	LORD	SKULL
CHIEF	FLAT	MAURICE	SPEAR
CLIFF	FOREST	MOUNTAIN	STONES
CONCH	GLASSES	OFFICER	SUN
CONFLICT	GOLDING	PIGGY	WOOD
COOPERATION	GOOD	PLAY	
CORPSE	GRIN	RAIN	
CRY	HESITATES	RALPH	

Lord of the Flies Word Search 4 Answer Key

ADULTS	DANCE	HIDE	ROCK
AIRPLANE	DARKNESS	HUNTERS	SAVAGE
BOULDER	FACE	JACK	SEA
CANDLE	FEAR	LITTLUNS	SIMON
CASTLE	FIRE	LORD	SKULL
CHIEF	FLAT	MAURICE	SPEAR
CLIFF	FOREST	MOUNTAIN	STONES
CONCH	GLASSES	OFFICER	SUN
CONFLICT	GOLDING	PIGGY	WOOD
COOPERATION	GOOD	PLAY	
CORPSE	GRIN	RAIN	
CRY	HESITATES	RALPH	

Lord of the Flies Crossword 1

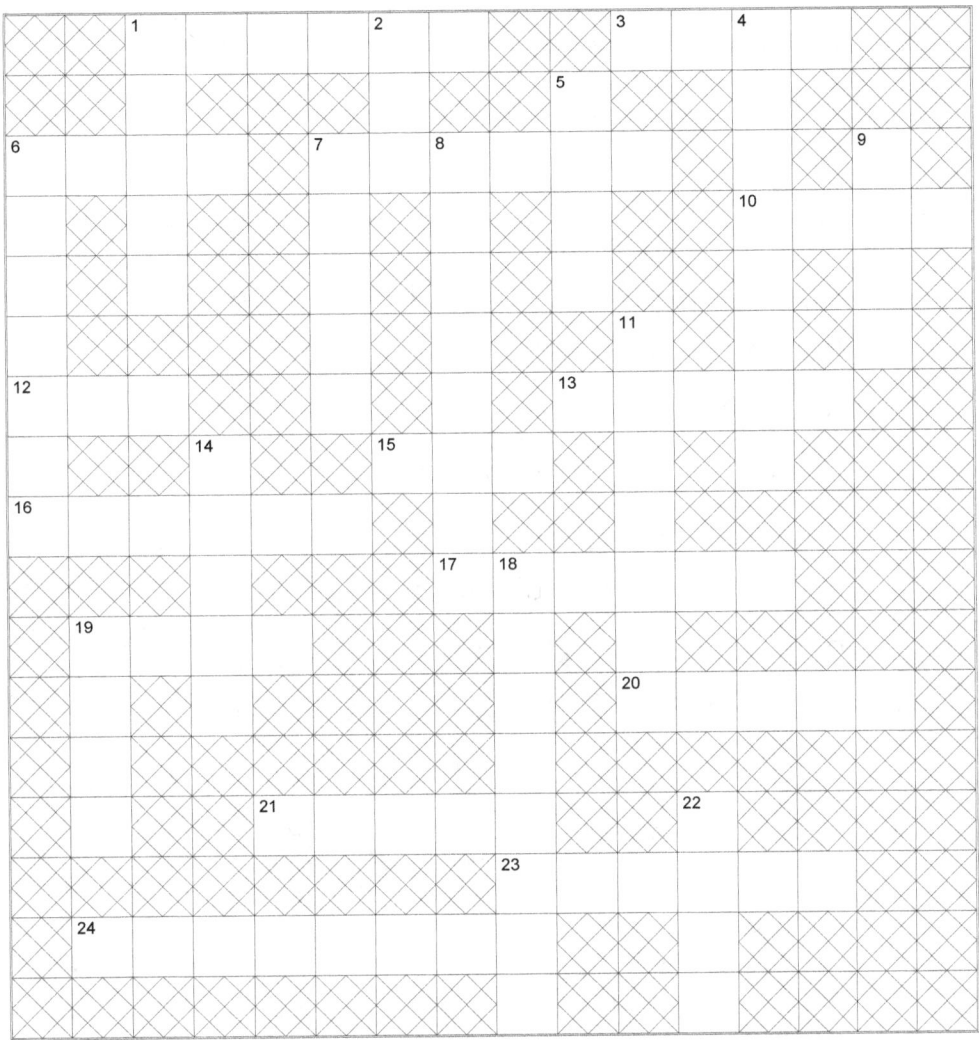

Across
1. Sam and Eric see the _____ of a parachutist
3. Jack paints his with clay
6. Expression on pig's face
7. Maurice and Roger destroy the Littluns' sand _____
10. Feeling the Littluns had
12. The boys used the _____'s rays to start a fire
13. Shell, symbol of authority
15. Sob
16. An animal man
17. Jack slashed the green _____ buds
19. Castle _____
20. Handsome, athletic, natural leader
21. Ralph encounters a grinning pig's _____
23. There are no _____ on the island until the officer arrives
24. Place from which the boys see something like a great ape

Down
1. Simon falls off one to the sands below
2. The bodies of Simon and the parachutist are carried out to _____
4. Man vs. man, for example
5. Shape of the rock on which Piggy lands
6. The boys use Piggy's _____ to start the fire
7. Another name for leader
8. Sam and Eric; identical twins
9. Choir leader, ugly without silliness
11. It shatters the conch and Piggy
14. The hunters' _____ was the act of killing
18. Boys' transportation to the island
19. Water from the sky
22. Jack announces to Ralph, I'm not going to _____ anymore. Not with you.

Lord of the Flies Crossword 1 Answer Key

	1 C	O	R	2 P S	E		3 F	A	4 C	E	
	L			E		5 F			O		
6 G	R	I	N	7 C	8 A	S	T	L	E	N	9 J
L		F		H	A				10 F	E	A	R
A		F		I	M		T		L		C	
S				E	N		11 B		I		K	
12 S	U	N		F		E		13 C	O	N	C	H
E		14 D		15 C	R	Y		U		T		
16 S	A	V	A	G	E		17 C	18 A	N	D	L	E
		N					I	R		E		
	19 R	O	C	K			I	20 R	A	L	P	H
	A		E					P				
	I				21 S	K	U	L	L		22 P	
	N							23 A	D	U	L	T	S
	24 M	O	U	N	T	A	I	N		A		
								E		Y		

Across
1. Sam and Eric see the _____ of a parachutist
3. Jack paints his with clay
6. Expression on pig's face
7. Maurice and Roger destroy the Littluns' sand _____
10. Feeling the Littluns had
12. The boys used the _____'s rays to start a fire
13. Shell, symbol of authority
15. Sob
16. An animal man
17. Jack slashed the green _____ buds
19. Castle _____
20. Handsome, athletic, natural leader
21. Ralph encounters a grinning pig's _____
23. There are no _____ on the island until the officer arrives
24. Place from which the boys see something like a great ape

Down
1. Simon falls off one to the sands below
2. The bodies of Simon and the parachutist are carried out to _____
4. Man vs. man, for example
5. Shape of the rock on which Piggy lands
6. The boys use Piggy's _____ to start the fire
7. Another name for leader
8. Sam and Eric; identical twins
9. Choir leader, ugly without silliness
11. It shatters the conch and Piggy
14. The hunters' _____ was the act of killing
18. Boys' transportation to the island
19. Water from the sky
22. Jack announces to Ralph, I'm not going to _____ anymore. Not with you.

Lord of the Flies Crossword 2

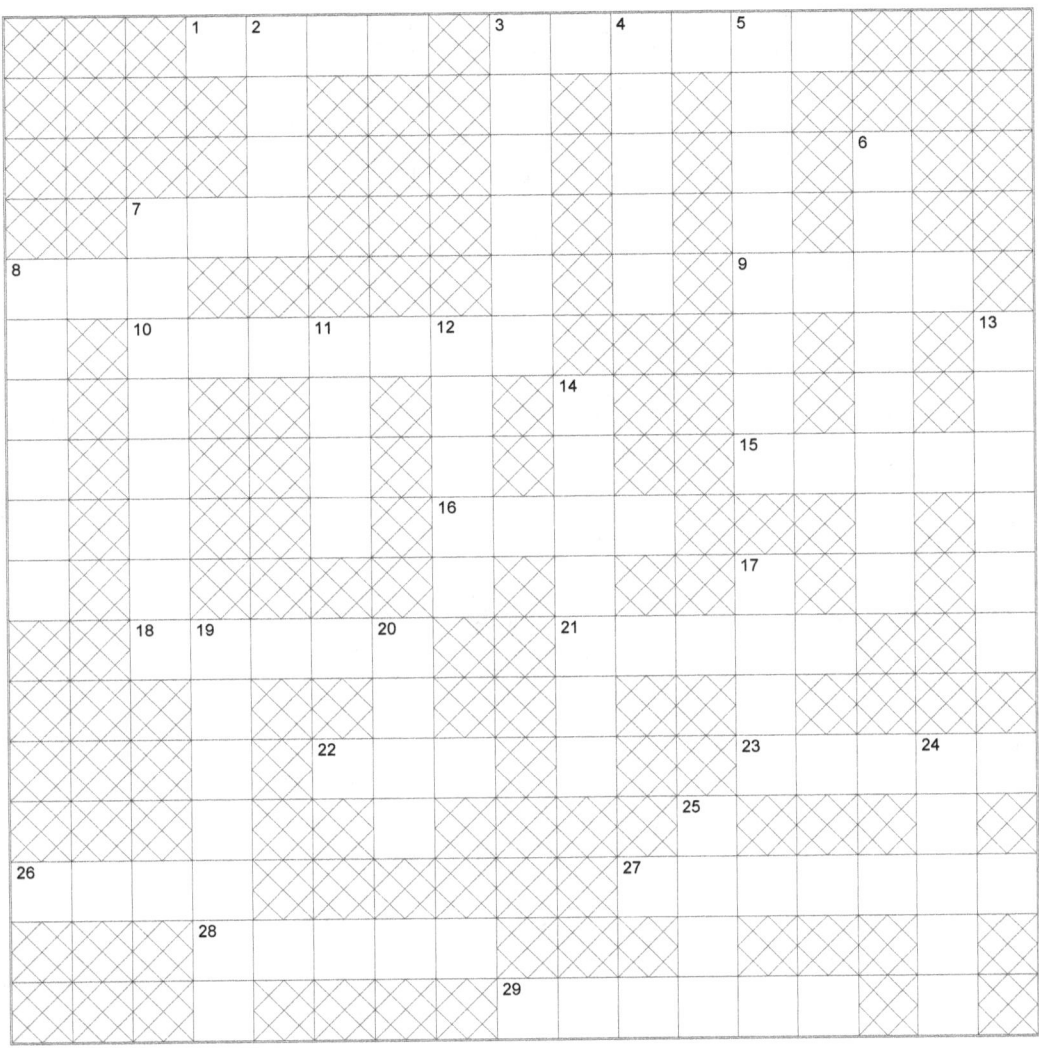

Across
1. Expression on pig's face
3. Maurice and Roger destroy the Littluns' sand _____
7. The boys used the _____'s rays to start a fire
8. The bodies of Simon and the parachutist are carried out to _____
9. _____ of the Flies
10. Choir boy as big as Jack, grinning all the time
15. Pointed stick
16. Shape of the rock on which Piggy lands
18. Another name for leader
21. Poetic, sensitive, loner, mysterious boy
22. Sob
23. The hunters' _____ was the act of killing
26. Conceal
27. Author
28. Handsome, athletic, natural leader
29. Jack slashed the green _____ buds

Down
2. Water from the sky
3. Sam and Eric see the _____ of a parachutist
4. Ralph encounters a grinning pig's _____
5. Name given to the numerous little children of the group
6. Symbolic of evil
7. Sam and Eric; identical twins
8. An animal man
11. Castle _____
12. Simon falls off one to the sands below
13. Thickly wooded area
14. The boys use Piggy's _____ to start the fire
17. It had to be collected to burn
19. The choir boys become this; responsible for getting food
20. Jack plans to steal it from Ralph and Piggy
24. Shell, symbol of authority
25. _____ vs. evil

Lord of the Flies Crossword 2 Answer Key

		1 G	2 R	I	N		3 C	4 A	5 S	T	L	E		
			A				O	K	I					
			I				R	U	T			6 D		
	7 S	U	N				P	L	T			A		
8 S	E	A					S	L	9 L	O	R	D		
A		10 M	A	U	11 R	I	12 C	E		U		K	13 F	
V		N			O		L	14 G		N		N	O	
A		E			C		L	L		15 S	P	E	A	R
G		R			K		16 F	L	A	T		S		E
E		I					F	S		17 W		S		S
	18 C	19 H	I	E	20 F		21 S	I	M	O	N			T
	U				I		E			O				
	N		22 C	R	Y		S			23 D	A	24 N	C	E
	T				E				25 G			O		
26 H	I	D	E					27 G	O	L	D	I	N	G
			28 R	A	L	P	H		O			C		
			S				29 C	A	N	D	L	E		H

Across
1. Expression on pig's face
3. Maurice and Roger destroy the Littluns' sand _____
7. The boys used the _____'s rays to start a fire
8. The bodies of Simon and the parachutist are carried out to _____
9. _____ of the Flies
10. Choir boy as big as Jack, grinning all the time
15. Pointed stick
16. Shape of the rock on which Piggy lands
18. Another name for leader
21. Poetic, sensitive, loner, mysterious boy
22. Sob
23. The hunters' _____ was the act of killing
26. Conceal
27. Author
28. Handsome, athletic, natural leader
29. Jack slashed the green _____ buds

Down
2. Water from the sky
3. Sam and Eric see the _____ of a parachutist
4. Ralph encounters a grinning pig's _____
5. Name given to the numerous little children of the group
6. Symbolic of evil
7. Sam and Eric; identical twins
8. An animal man
11. Castle _____
12. Simon falls off one to the sands below
13. Thickly wooded area
14. The boys use Piggy's _____ to start the fire
17. It had to be collected to burn
19. The choir boys become this; responsible for getting food
20. Jack plans to steal it from Ralph and Piggy
24. Shell, symbol of authority
25. _____ vs. evil

Lord of the Flies Crossword 3

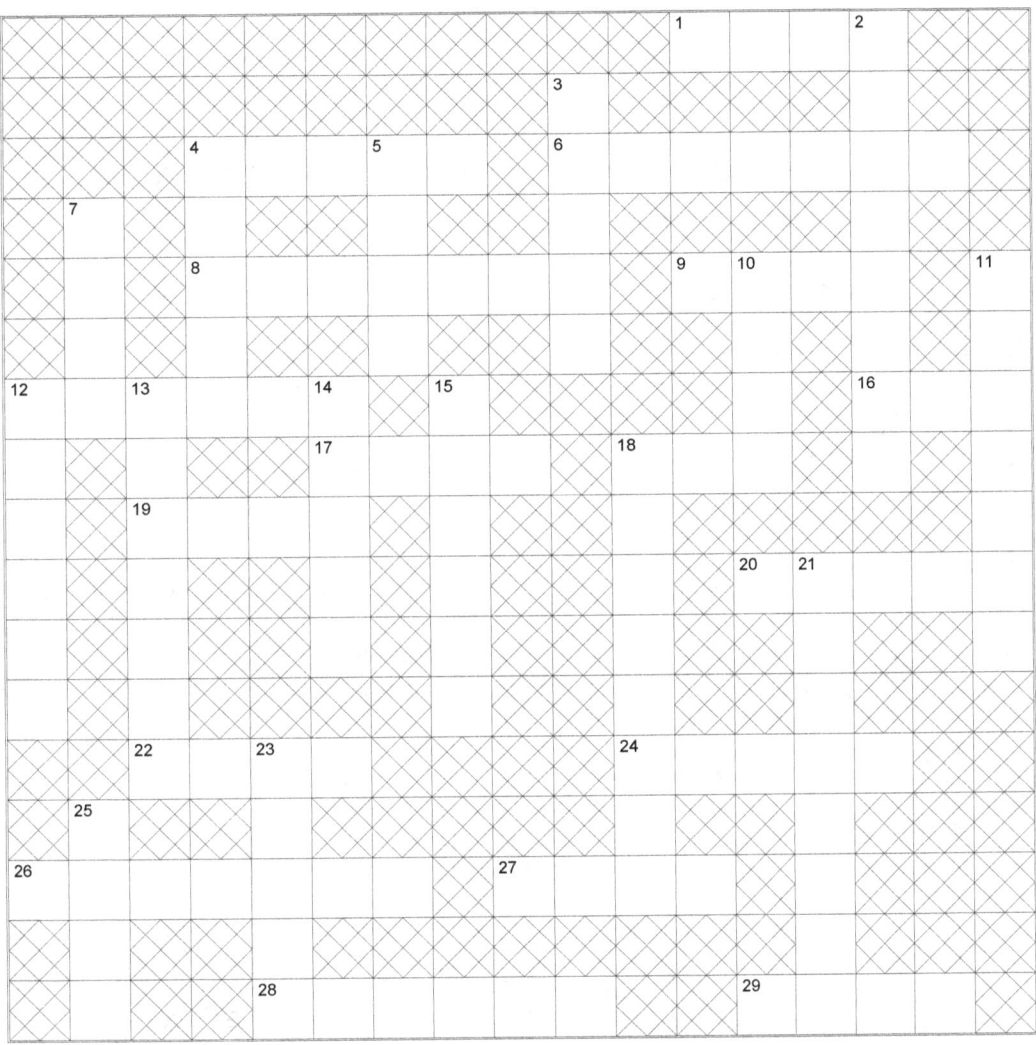

Across
1. It had to be collected to burn
4. Ralph encounters a grinning pig's _____
6. The choir boys become this; responsible for getting food
8. Choir boy as big as Jack, grinning all the time
9. Expression on pig's face
12. Roger stalks Henry and throws these near him
16. The bodies of Simon and the parachutist are carried out to _____
17. Jack announces to Ralph, I'm not going to _____ anymore. Not with you.
18. The boys used the _____'s rays to start a fire
19. Jack plans to steal it from Ralph and Piggy
20. The hunters' _____ was the act of killing
22. Castle _____
24. Handsome, athletic, natural leader
26. Author
27. Choir leader, ugly without silliness
28. Thickly wooded area
29. Feeling the Littluns had

Down
2. Symbolic of evil
3. Another name for leader
4. Poetic, sensitive, loner, mysterious boy
5. _____ of the Flies
7. Shape of the rock on which Piggy lands
10. Water from the sky
11. The boys use Piggy's _____ to start the fire
12. An animal man
13. A British naval _____ saves Ralph
14. Pointed stick
15. Maurice and Roger destroy the Littluns' sand _____
18. Sam and Eric; identical twins
21. Boys' transportation to the island
23. Simon falls off one to the sands below
25. _____ vs. evil

Lord of the Flies Crossword 3 Answer Key

											¹W	O	O	²D	
								³C						A	
			⁴S	K	U	⁵L	L	⁶H	U	N	T	E	R	S	
	⁷F		I			O		I						K	
	L		⁸M	A	U	R	I	C	E		⁹G	¹⁰R	I	N	¹¹G
	A		O			D		F			A	E			L
¹²S	T	¹³O	N	¹⁴E	S	¹⁵C					I		¹⁶S	E	A
A		F		¹⁷P	L	A	Y		¹⁸S	U	N		S		S
V		¹⁹F	I	R	E	S			A				S		S
A		I		A		T			M		²⁰D	²¹A	N	C	E
G		C		R		L			N		I				S
E		E				E			E		R				
	²²R	O	²³C	K				²⁴R	A	L	P	H			
²⁵G			L					I			L				
²⁶G	O	L	D	I	N	G		²⁷J	A	C	K				
O			F								A				
D			²⁸F	O	R	E	S	T		²⁹F	E	A	R		

Across
1. It had to be collected to burn
4. Ralph encounters a grinning pig's _____
6. The choir boys become this; responsible for getting food
8. Choir boy as big as Jack, grinning all the time
9. Expression on pig's face
12. Roger stalks Henry and throws these near him
16. The bodies of Simon and the parachutist are carried out to _____
17. Jack announces to Ralph, I'm not going to _____ anymore. Not with you.
18. The boys used the _____'s rays to start a fire
19. Jack plans to steal it from Ralph and Piggy
20. The hunters' _____ was the act of killing
22. Castle _____
24. Handsome, athletic, natural leader
26. Author
27. Choir leader, ugly without silliness
28. Thickly wooded area
29. Feeling the Littluns had

Down
2. Symbolic of evil
3. Another name for leader
4. Poetic, sensitive, loner, mysterious boy
5. _____ of the Flies
7. Shape of the rock on which Piggy lands
10. Water from the sky
11. The boys use Piggy's _____ to start the fire
12. An animal man
13. A British naval _____ saves Ralph
14. Pointed stick
15. Maurice and Roger destroy the Littluns' sand _____
18. Sam and Eric; identical twins
21. Boys' transportation to the island
23. Simon falls off one to the sands below
25. _____ vs. evil

Lord of the Flies Crossword 4

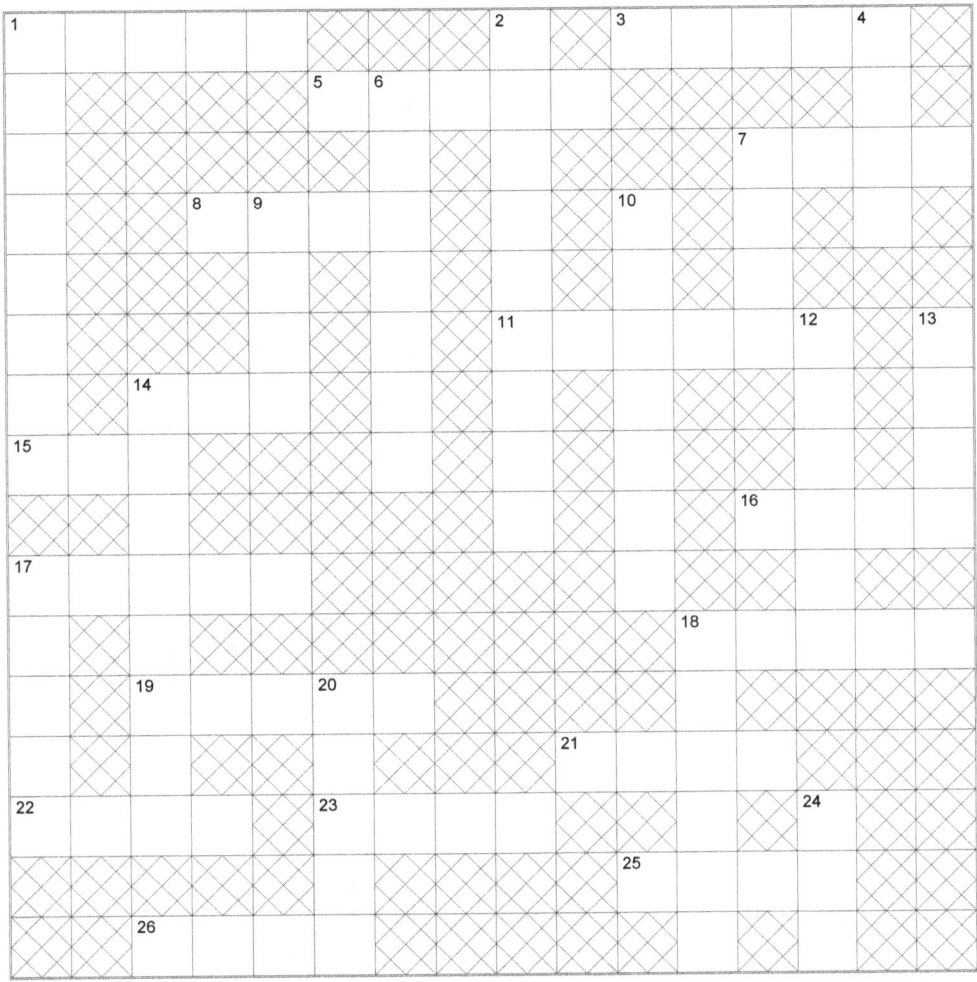

Across
1. The hunters' _____ was the act of killing
3. Ralph encounters a grinning pig's _____
5. Another name for leader
7. Jack plans to steal it from Ralph and Piggy
8. Expression on pig's face
11. There are no _____ on the island until the officer arrives
14. The boys used the _____'s rays to start a fire
15. The bodies of Simon and the parachutist are carried out to _____
16. Choir leader, ugly without silliness
17. Shell, symbol of authority
18. Pointed stick
19. Handsome, athletic, natural leader
21. It had to be collected to burn
22. Jack paints his with clay
23. _____ vs. evil
25. Feeling the Littluns had
26. Jack announces to Ralph, I'm not going to _____ anymore. Not with you.

Down
1. Symbolic of evil
2. Jack does this when he lifts his knife to kill the piglet
4. _____ of the Flies
6. The choir boys become this; responsible for getting food
7. Shape of the rock on which Piggy lands
9. Water from the sky
10. Choir boy as big as Jack, grinning all the time
12. An animal man
13. Castle _____
14. Sam and Eric; identical twins
17. Simon falls off one to the sands below
18. Roger stalks Henry and throws these near him
20. Intelligent, reader and thinker rather than a boy of action
24. Sob

Lord of the Flies Crossword 4 Answer Key

	1 D	A	N	C	E			2 H		3 S	K	U	L	4 L	
	A					5 C	6 H	I	E	F				O	
	R					U		S				7 F	I	R	E
	K		8 G	9 R	I	N		I		10 M		L		D	
	N			A		T		T		A		A			
	E			I		E		11 A	D	U	L	12 T	S	13 R	
	S	14 S	U	N		R		T		R		A		O	
15 S	E	A				S		E		I		V		C	
		M						S		C		16 J	A	C	K
17 C	O	N	C	H				E				G			
L		E								18 S	P	E	A	R	
I		19 R	A	20 L	P	H				T					
F		I		I				21 W	O	O	D				
22 F	A	C	E		23 G	O	O	D		N		24 C			
				G						25 F	E	A	R		
		26 P	L	A	Y					S		Y			

Across
1. The hunters' _____ was the act of killing
3. Ralph encounters a grinning pig's _____
5. Another name for leader
7. Jack plans to steal it from Ralph and Piggy
8. Expression on pig's face
11. There are no _____ on the island until the officer arrives
14. The boys used the _____'s rays to start a fire
15. The bodies of Simon and the parachutist are carried out to _____
16. Choir leader, ugly without silliness
17. Shell, symbol of authority
18. Pointed stick
19. Handsome, athletic, natural leader
21. It had to be collected to burn
22. Jack paints his with clay
23. _____ vs. evil
25. Feeling the Littluns had
26. Jack announces to Ralph, I'm not going to _____ anymore. Not with you.

Down
1. Symbolic of evil
2. Jack does this when he lifts his knife to kill the piglet
4. _____ of the Flies
6. The choir boys become this; responsible for getting food
7. Shape of the rock on which Piggy lands
9. Water from the sky
10. Choir boy as big as Jack, grinning all the time
12. An animal man
13. Castle _____
14. Sam and Eric; identical twins
17. Simon falls off one to the sands below
18. Roger stalks Henry and throws these near him
20. Intelligent, reader and thinker rather than a boy of action
24. Sob

Lord of the Flies

SAVAGE	CORPSE	CHIEF	RALPH	DARKNESS
SIMON	SEA	MAURICE	STONES	PIGGY
LITTLUNS	MOUNTAIN	FREE SPACE	WOOD	CONCH
JACK	OFFICER	HIDE	SKULL	SPEAR
BOULDER	PLAY	CANDLE	SUN	CLIFF

Lord of the Flies

COOPERATION	RAIN	FACE	FLAT	CONFLICT
LORD	GLASSES	CASTLE	HUNTERS	FEAR
FOREST	SAMNERIC	FREE SPACE	ROCK	AIRPLANE
ADULTS	FIRE	DANCE	CRY	GOOD
GRIN	CLIFF	SUN	CANDLE	PLAY

Lord of the Flies

CHIEF	MAURICE	HESITATES	SAMNERIC	RAIN
ROCK	CANDLE	GOOD	FOREST	PIGGY
FEAR	OFFICER	FREE SPACE	STONES	BOULDER
SKULL	LORD	WOOD	GRIN	FLAT
CLIFF	SPEAR	PLAY	RALPH	FACE

Lord of the Flies

LITTLUNS	MOUNTAIN	FIRE	CONFLICT	GOLDING
DANCE	DARKNESS	SEA	COOPERATION	SIMON
SAVAGE	GLASSES	FREE SPACE	JACK	CASTLE
CRY	HIDE	AIRPLANE	CONCH	CORPSE
SUN	FACE	RALPH	PLAY	SPEAR

Lord of the Flies

ADULTS	GOLDING	DARKNESS	PLAY	PIGGY
RAIN	FIRE	FLAT	GLASSES	MOUNTAIN
CONFLICT	HUNTERS	FREE SPACE	CHIEF	SAVAGE
SKULL	RALPH	LORD	ROCK	OFFICER
DANCE	GOOD	JACK	FACE	SAMNERIC

Lord of the Flies

SIMON	SPEAR	WOOD	COOPERATION	LITTLUNS
GRIN	AIRPLANE	MAURICE	STONES	SEA
CRY	CONCH	FREE SPACE	BOULDER	FEAR
CANDLE	CASTLE	CLIFF	SUN	HESITATES
CORPSE	SAMNERIC	FACE	JACK	GOOD

Lord of the Flies

RALPH	SUN	DANCE	CORPSE	LORD
CLIFF	STONES	CONCH	JACK	ROCK
RAIN	HUNTERS	FREE SPACE	GOLDING	SKULL
BOULDER	FLAT	SAVAGE	PLAY	LITTLUNS
FOREST	ADULTS	FACE	SPEAR	WOOD

Lord of the Flies

CASTLE	COOPERATION	MOUNTAIN	CHIEF	CRY
HIDE	SEA	SIMON	HESITATES	OFFICER
DARKNESS	GLASSES	FREE SPACE	GRIN	CONFLICT
GOOD	SAMNERIC	PIGGY	MAURICE	FEAR
CANDLE	WOOD	SPEAR	FACE	ADULTS

Lord of the Flies

LORD	SPEAR	RAIN	CLIFF	SAVAGE
GOLDING	FOREST	FACE	PIGGY	RALPH
SUN	LITTLUNS	FREE SPACE	HIDE	SKULL
FEAR	CONFLICT	MOUNTAIN	PLAY	JACK
OFFICER	ADULTS	CANDLE	FLAT	GOOD

Lord of the Flies

SIMON	BOULDER	DANCE	CRY	CORPSE
CHIEF	COOPERATION	STONES	DARKNESS	CONCH
HESITATES	WOOD	FREE SPACE	GLASSES	SAMNERIC
ROCK	HUNTERS	FIRE	GRIN	AIRPLANE
SEA	GOOD	FLAT	CANDLE	ADULTS

Lord of the Flies

BOULDER	CORPSE	MAURICE	CANDLE	JACK
CONFLICT	AIRPLANE	GOLDING	FLAT	HESITATES
STONES	HIDE	FREE SPACE	FEAR	RAIN
HUNTERS	CRY	SEA	GRIN	SUN
SPEAR	COOPERATION	SAMNERIC	GLASSES	GOOD

Lord of the Flies

FOREST	CHIEF	SAVAGE	ROCK	SIMON
OFFICER	LORD	WOOD	FIRE	CONCH
MOUNTAIN	PLAY	FREE SPACE	ADULTS	CLIFF
DANCE	LITTLUNS	PIGGY	FACE	RALPH
SKULL	GOOD	GLASSES	SAMNERIC	COOPERATION

Lord of the Flies

PIGGY	COOPERATION	LITTLUNS	CLIFF	GRIN
AIRPLANE	SAMNERIC	CANDLE	SAVAGE	GOLDING
FACE	CORPSE	FREE SPACE	CONFLICT	SEA
OFFICER	MOUNTAIN	GLASSES	GOOD	HESITATES
CHIEF	JACK	SKULL	STONES	FEAR

Lord of the Flies

BOULDER	FLAT	SUN	CONCH	WOOD
MAURICE	FOREST	ROCK	RAIN	CRY
RALPH	HUNTERS	FREE SPACE	CASTLE	ADULTS
SIMON	FIRE	DARKNESS	HIDE	LORD
DANCE	FEAR	STONES	SKULL	JACK

Lord of the Flies

DANCE	HIDE	BOULDER	SAVAGE	ROCK
PIGGY	WOOD	SAMNERIC	OFFICER	HESITATES
FEAR	CONFLICT	FREE SPACE	JACK	GLASSES
FLAT	CRY	CASTLE	ADULTS	RALPH
CONCH	CHIEF	FIRE	DARKNESS	CLIFF

Lord of the Flies

SEA	LORD	AIRPLANE	CANDLE	MAURICE
SKULL	GRIN	GOOD	RAIN	COOPERATION
FOREST	FACE	FREE SPACE	SUN	LITTLUNS
SPEAR	GOLDING	CORPSE	MOUNTAIN	STONES
SIMON	CLIFF	DARKNESS	FIRE	CHIEF

Lord of the Flies

GOOD	MAURICE	SPEAR	HUNTERS	SEA
WOOD	SUN	CRY	JACK	GLASSES
PLAY	SAVAGE	FREE SPACE	ROCK	CANDLE
BOULDER	FACE	CONCH	FLAT	STONES
FEAR	PIGGY	HIDE	RAIN	CASTLE

Lord of the Flies

FOREST	ADULTS	FIRE	SKULL	SIMON
AIRPLANE	CONFLICT	DARKNESS	HESITATES	COOPERATION
CHIEF	OFFICER	FREE SPACE	SAMNERIC	MOUNTAIN
LITTLUNS	CORPSE	LORD	CLIFF	DANCE
GOLDING	CASTLE	RAIN	HIDE	PIGGY

Lord of the Flies

CANDLE	ADULTS	HIDE	JACK	GRIN
AIRPLANE	SIMON	CONFLICT	OFFICER	FLAT
GLASSES	LITTLUNS	FREE SPACE	CHIEF	RALPH
MOUNTAIN	MAURICE	RAIN	ROCK	COOPERATION
SUN	SEA	HUNTERS	DARKNESS	SPEAR

Lord of the Flies

FACE	FEAR	SAVAGE	PLAY	GOOD
CORPSE	BOULDER	CONCH	FOREST	CASTLE
LORD	FIRE	FREE SPACE	GOLDING	CRY
SAMNERIC	WOOD	CLIFF	STONES	DANCE
SKULL	SPEAR	DARKNESS	HUNTERS	SEA

Lord of the Flies

GLASSES	GRIN	SPEAR	CORPSE	AIRPLANE
CRY	FIRE	FACE	ADULTS	LORD
SAVAGE	FEAR	FREE SPACE	PIGGY	JACK
GOLDING	FLAT	OFFICER	FOREST	DARKNESS
HIDE	SUN	STONES	CASTLE	COOPERATION

Lord of the Flies

SKULL	RAIN	CONFLICT	BOULDER	MOUNTAIN
PLAY	SAMNERIC	CONCH	CLIFF	LITTLUNS
WOOD	HESITATES	FREE SPACE	RALPH	SEA
SIMON	GOOD	MAURICE	DANCE	CHIEF
HUNTERS	COOPERATION	CASTLE	STONES	SUN

Lord of the Flies

HUNTERS	CHIEF	LORD	DANCE	SAMNERIC
BOULDER	RAIN	ROCK	SKULL	AIRPLANE
SAVAGE	RALPH	FREE SPACE	PIGGY	SPEAR
FACE	CLIFF	CANDLE	CONCH	OFFICER
MOUNTAIN	JACK	FIRE	HESITATES	GOOD

Lord of the Flies

WOOD	SEA	COOPERATION	MAURICE	SIMON
LITTLUNS	FLAT	CASTLE	PLAY	CRY
GRIN	FEAR	FREE SPACE	ADULTS	GOLDING
CORPSE	HIDE	STONES	FOREST	CONFLICT
SUN	GOOD	HESITATES	FIRE	JACK

Lord of the Flies

FACE	SKULL	GLASSES	AIRPLANE	SIMON
CONFLICT	CASTLE	MOUNTAIN	FOREST	LORD
ROCK	DARKNESS	FREE SPACE	FLAT	LITTLUNS
CONCH	SAMNERIC	HUNTERS	BOULDER	RALPH
DANCE	HESITATES	MAURICE	RAIN	GOLDING

Lord of the Flies

COOPERATION	SEA	PIGGY	CHIEF	CORPSE
CLIFF	OFFICER	PLAY	FIRE	GOOD
GRIN	ADULTS	FREE SPACE	CRY	FEAR
WOOD	SUN	SPEAR	SAVAGE	HIDE
CANDLE	GOLDING	RAIN	MAURICE	HESITATES

Lord of the Flies

CRY	CASTLE	SPEAR	DARKNESS	PLAY
ADULTS	GRIN	CLIFF	MOUNTAIN	CONCH
LORD	RAIN	FREE SPACE	JACK	HESITATES
OFFICER	LITTLUNS	SUN	SAMNERIC	ROCK
AIRPLANE	FOREST	SAVAGE	RALPH	SIMON

Lord of the Flies

BOULDER	HUNTERS	GOOD	MAURICE	GLASSES
FLAT	FIRE	SKULL	HIDE	CORPSE
SEA	FACE	FREE SPACE	CONFLICT	FEAR
PIGGY	GOLDING	STONES	CHIEF	DANCE
CANDLE	SIMON	RALPH	SAVAGE	FOREST

Lord of the Flies

FACE	FIRE	HUNTERS	SUN	SAMNERIC
CRY	CASTLE	AIRPLANE	DARKNESS	GOOD
ADULTS	SKULL	FREE SPACE	GLASSES	GOLDING
GRIN	WOOD	SPEAR	JACK	CANDLE
HIDE	SIMON	CHIEF	OFFICER	MOUNTAIN

Lord of the Flies

CONCH	PLAY	RAIN	CLIFF	FOREST
LITTLUNS	FLAT	FEAR	BOULDER	MAURICE
LORD	SEA	FREE SPACE	COOPERATION	HESITATES
SAVAGE	STONES	CORPSE	CONFLICT	DANCE
ROCK	MOUNTAIN	OFFICER	CHIEF	SIMON

Lord of the Flies

SPEAR	SAMNERIC	PIGGY	HESITATES	SUN
RALPH	RAIN	FIRE	HIDE	STONES
HUNTERS	GRIN	FREE SPACE	BOULDER	CONCH
PLAY	CRY	GOLDING	DARKNESS	FOREST
CASTLE	COOPERATION	LITTLUNS	CHIEF	MAURICE

Lord of the Flies

FEAR	FLAT	CORPSE	LORD	JACK
DANCE	SAVAGE	GOOD	MOUNTAIN	WOOD
FACE	CLIFF	FREE SPACE	CONFLICT	ROCK
CANDLE	SKULL	SEA	GLASSES	OFFICER
SIMON	MAURICE	CHIEF	LITTLUNS	COOPERATION

Lord of the Flies Vocabulary Word List

No.	Word	Clue/Definition
1.	APEX	The highest point
2.	ASSIMILATING	Absorbing
3.	BASTION	A well-fortified position
4.	COVERTS	Thick underbrush providing cover
5.	CREPITATION	Crackling sound
6.	CYNICISM	Attitude scornful of the motives or virtues of others
7.	DECLIVITIES	Downward slopes
8.	DERISION	Scorn or ridicule
9.	DERISIVE	Scornful
10.	EBULLIENCE	Zestful enthusiasm
11.	ECLIPSED	Obscured; blocked from view
12.	EFFIGY	A likeness or image
13.	ELEPHANTINE	Ponderously clumsy
14.	EXCRUCIATINGLY	Intensely painfully
15.	FESTOONED	Decorated
16.	GESTICULATED	Made hand motions
17.	GLAMOUR	Magic spell; enchantment
18.	HIATUS	A break
19.	IMPALPABLE	Intangible; not perceived by touch
20.	IMPERVIOUS	Incapable of being affected
21.	IMPROVISATION	To invent without preparation
22.	INCANTATION	A verbal charm or spell
23.	INCREDULITY	Disbelief
24.	INIMICAL	Unfriendly; hostile
25.	INSCRUTABLE	Impenetrable
26.	LUXURIANCE	Having rich or profuse growth
27.	MATERNAL	Relating to motherhood
28.	MYOPIA	A visual defect like nearsightedness
29.	OBTUSENESS	Dullness; flatness; lack of sharp edges
30.	OPAQUE	Light can't get through it
31.	PALL	A gloomy effect
32.	PINNACLES	Tall, pointed formations
33.	PROPITATINGLY	Appeasingly; trying to please
34.	PURGED	Freed from impurities
35.	REBUKE	To criticize or reprimand
36.	SANCTITY	Sacredness; godliness
37.	SINEWY	Lean and muscular
38.	SKEWED	Turned to one side
39.	SPECIOUS	Plausible but actually false
40.	TACITLY	Without being spoken
41.	TAUT	Tight
42.	TEMPESTUOUSLY	Like a storm; turbulently
43.	TRUCULENTLY	Disposed to fight

Lord of the Flies Vocabulary Fill In The Blank 1

_____ 1. To invent without preparation

_____ 2. Downward slopes

_____ 3. Disposed to fight

_____ 4. To criticize or reprimand

_____ 5. Intensely painfully

_____ 6. A break

_____ 7. Intangible; not perceived by touch

_____ 8. Obscured; blocked from view

_____ 9. Tall, pointed formations

_____ 10. Dullness; flatness; lack of sharp edges

_____ 11. Made hand motions

_____ 12. Sacredness; godliness

_____ 13. Light can't get through it

_____ 14. Decorated

_____ 15. Absorbing

_____ 16. Thick underbrush providing cover

_____ 17. Attitude scornful of the motives or virtues of others

_____ 18. A gloomy effect

_____ 19. A visual defect like nearsightedness

_____ 20. Like a storm; turbulently

Lord of the Flies Vocabulary Fill In The Blank 1 Answer Key

IMPROVISATION	1. To invent without preparation
DECLIVITIES	2. Downward slopes
TRUCULENTLY	3. Disposed to fight
REBUKE	4. To criticize or reprimand
EXCRUCIATINGLY	5. Intensely painfully
HIATUS	6. A break
IMPALPABLE	7. Intangible; not perceived by touch
ECLIPSED	8. Obscured; blocked from view
PINNACLES	9. Tall, pointed formations
OBTUSENESS	10. Dullness; flatness; lack of sharp edges
GESTICULATED	11. Made hand motions
SANCTITY	12. Sacredness; godliness
OPAQUE	13. Light can't get through it
FESTOONED	14. Decorated
ASSIMILATING	15. Absorbing
COVERTS	16. Thick underbrush providing cover
CYNICISM	17. Attitude scornful of the motives or virtues of others
PALL	18. A gloomy effect
MYOPIA	19. A visual defect like nearsightedness
TEMPESTUOUSLY	20. Like a storm; turbulently

Lord of the Flies Vocabulary Fill In The Blank 2

_____   1. Ponderously clumsy

_____   2. Thick underbrush providing cover

_____   3. Sacredness; godliness

_____   4. Zestful enthusiasm

_____   5. Having rich or profuse growth

_____   6. Freed from impurities

_____   7. Downward slopes

_____   8. Magic spell; enchantment

_____   9. Decorated

_____   10. Tight

_____   11. To criticize or reprimand

_____   12. Appeasingly; trying to please

_____   13. Scorn or ridicule

_____   14. Tall, pointed formations

_____   15. Intangible; not perceived by touch

_____   16. Plausible but actually false

_____   17. Disposed to fight

_____   18. A likeness or image

_____   19. Unfriendly; hostile

_____   20. Light can't get through it

Lord of the Flies Vocabulary Fill In The Blank 2 Answer Key

ELEPHANTINE	1. Ponderously clumsy
COVERTS	2. Thick underbrush providing cover
SANCTITY	3. Sacredness; godliness
EBULLIENCE	4. Zestful enthusiasm
LUXURIANCE	5. Having rich or profuse growth
PURGED	6. Freed from impurities
DECLIVITIES	7. Downward slopes
GLAMOUR	8. Magic spell; enchantment
FESTOONED	9. Decorated
TAUT	10. Tight
REBUKE	11. To criticize or reprimand
PROPITATINGLY	12. Appeasingly; trying to please
DERISION	13. Scorn or ridicule
PINNACLES	14. Tall, pointed formations
IMPALPABLE	15. Intangible; not perceived by touch
SPECIOUS	16. Plausible but actually false
TRUCULENTLY	17. Disposed to fight
EFFIGY	18. A likeness or image
INIMICAL	19. Unfriendly; hostile
OPAQUE	20. Light can't get through it

Lord of the Flies Vocabulary Fill In The Blank 3

_____ 1. Obscured; blocked from view

_____ 2. Light can't get through it

_____ 3. A break

_____ 4. Attitude scornful of the motives or virtues of others

_____ 5. Impenetrable

_____ 6. Appeasingly; trying to please

_____ 7. A visual defect like nearsightedness

_____ 8. Disbelief

_____ 9. Scorn or ridicule

_____ 10. Turned to one side

_____ 11. Decorated

_____ 12. A verbal charm or spell

_____ 13. Scornful

_____ 14. Absorbing

_____ 15. To criticize or reprimand

_____ 16. Downward slopes

_____ 17. Thick underbrush providing cover

_____ 18. Zestful enthusiasm

_____ 19. Without being spoken

_____ 20. To invent without preparation

Lord of the Flies Vocabulary Fill In The Blank 3 Answer Key

ECLIPSED	1. Obscured; blocked from view
OPAQUE	2. Light can't get through it
HIATUS	3. A break
CYNICISM	4. Attitude scornful of the motives or virtues of others
INSCRUTABLE	5. Impenetrable
PROPITATINGLY	6. Appeasingly; trying to please
MYOPIA	7. A visual defect like nearsightedness
INCREDULITY	8. Disbelief
DERISION	9. Scorn or ridicule
SKEWED	10. Turned to one side
FESTOONED	11. Decorated
INCANTATION	12. A verbal charm or spell
DERISIVE	13. Scornful
ASSIMILATING	14. Absorbing
REBUKE	15. To criticize or reprimand
DECLIVITIES	16. Downward slopes
COVERTS	17. Thick underbrush providing cover
EBULLIENCE	18. Zestful enthusiasm
TACITLY	19. Without being spoken
IMPROVISATION	20. To invent without preparation

Lord of the Flies Vocabulary Fill In The Blank 4

_____ 1. Turned to one side

_____ 2. A well-fortified position

_____ 3. Incapable of being affected

_____ 4. A visual defect like nearsightedness

_____ 5. Ponderously clumsy

_____ 6. Magic spell; enchantment

_____ 7. Scorn or ridicule

_____ 8. Having rich or profuse growth

_____ 9. Relating to motherhood

_____ 10. Appeasingly; trying to please

_____ 11. Attitude scornful of the motives or virtues of others

_____ 12. Thick underbrush providing cover

_____ 13. Lean and muscular

_____ 14. Zestful enthusiasm

_____ 15. A break

_____ 16. Like a storm; turbulently

_____ 17. Disposed to fight

_____ 18. Intensely painfully

_____ 19. Made hand motions

_____ 20. To criticize or reprimand

Lord of the Flies Vocabulary Fill In The Blank 4 Answer Key

SKEWED	1. Turned to one side
BASTION	2. A well-fortified position
IMPERVIOUS	3. Incapable of being affected
MYOPIA	4. A visual defect like nearsightedness
ELEPHANTINE	5. Ponderously clumsy
GLAMOUR	6. Magic spell; enchantment
DERISION	7. Scorn or ridicule
LUXURIANCE	8. Having rich or profuse growth
MATERNAL	9. Relating to motherhood
PROPITATINGLY	10. Appeasingly; trying to please
CYNICISM	11. Attitude scornful of the motives or virtues of others
COVERTS	12. Thick underbrush providing cover
SINEWY	13. Lean and muscular
EBULLIENCE	14. Zestful enthusiasm
HIATUS	15. A break
TEMPESTUOUSLY	16. Like a storm; turbulently
TRUCULENTLY	17. Disposed to fight
EXCRUCIATINGLY	18. Intensely painfully
GESTICULATED	19. Made hand motions
REBUKE	20. To criticize or reprimand

Lord of the Flies Vocabulary Matching 1

___ 1. OBTUSENESS   A. Downward slopes
___ 2. IMPROVISATION   B. Scornful
___ 3. PURGED   C. Magic spell; enchantment
___ 4. OPAQUE   D. Disbelief
___ 5. TAUT   E. Dullness; flatness; lack of sharp edges
___ 6. ASSIMILATING   F. A verbal charm or spell
___ 7. FESTOONED   G. Decorated
___ 8. PALL   H. Thick underbrush providing cover
___ 9. SANCTITY   I. Turned to one side
___10. DECLIVITIES   J. Lean and muscular
___11. INIMICAL   K. Relating to motherhood
___12. SPECIOUS   L. A gloomy effect
___13. APEX   M. Unfriendly; hostile
___14. DERISIVE   N. Light can't get through it
___15. INCANTATION   O. Impenetrable
___16. SKEWED   P. Freed from impurities
___17. COVERTS   Q. Sacredness; godliness
___18. TEMPESTUOUSLY   R. Tight
___19. REBUKE   S. Plausible but actually false
___20. INSCRUTABLE   T. Absorbing
___21. SINEWY   U. To invent without preparation
___22. GLAMOUR   V. Tall, pointed formations
___23. PINNACLES   W. To criticize or reprimand
___24. INCREDULITY   X. The highest point
___25. MATERNAL   Y. Like a storm; turbulently

Lord of the Flies Vocabulary Matching 1 Answer Key

E - 1.	OBTUSENESS	A. Downward slopes
U - 2.	IMPROVISATION	B. Scornful
P - 3.	PURGED	C. Magic spell; enchantment
N - 4.	OPAQUE	D. Disbelief
R - 5.	TAUT	E. Dullness; flatness; lack of sharp edges
T - 6.	ASSIMILATING	F. A verbal charm or spell
G - 7.	FESTOONED	G. Decorated
L - 8.	PALL	H. Thick underbrush providing cover
Q - 9.	SANCTITY	I. Turned to one side
A - 10.	DECLIVITIES	J. Lean and muscular
M - 11.	INIMICAL	K. Relating to motherhood
S - 12.	SPECIOUS	L. A gloomy effect
X - 13.	APEX	M. Unfriendly; hostile
B - 14.	DERISIVE	N. Light can't get through it
F - 15.	INCANTATION	O. Impenetrable
I - 16.	SKEWED	P. Freed from impurities
H - 17.	COVERTS	Q. Sacredness; godliness
Y - 18.	TEMPESTUOUSLY	R. Tight
W - 19.	REBUKE	S. Plausible but actually false
O - 20.	INSCRUTABLE	T. Absorbing
J - 21.	SINEWY	U. To invent without preparation
C - 22.	GLAMOUR	V. Tall, pointed formations
V - 23.	PINNACLES	W. To criticize or reprimand
D - 24.	INCREDULITY	X. The highest point
K - 25.	MATERNAL	Y. Like a storm; turbulently

Lord of the Flies Vocabulary Matching 2

___ 1. PALL   A. Thick underbrush providing cover
___ 2. BASTION   B. A gloomy effect
___ 3. INCREDULITY   C. Relating to motherhood
___ 4. HIATUS   D. Made hand motions
___ 5. CYNICISM   E. Scorn or ridicule
___ 6. INIMICAL   F. Scornful
___ 7. SPECIOUS   G. Attitude scornful of the motives or virtues of others
___ 8. PURGED   H. Ponderously clumsy
___ 9. ELEPHANTINE   I. Impenetrable
___ 10. MATERNAL   J. Crackling sound
___ 11. GLAMOUR   K. Absorbing
___ 12. DERISIVE   L. Intangible; not perceived by touch
___ 13. GESTICULATED   M. A likeness or image
___ 14. DERISION   N. A well-fortified position
___ 15. INSCRUTABLE   O. Plausible but actually false
___ 16. OPAQUE   P. Disbelief
___ 17. CREPITATION   Q. Incapable of being affected
___ 18. ECLIPSED   R. Lean and muscular
___ 19. IMPROVISATION   S. Freed from impurities
___ 20. COVERTS   T. A break
___ 21. IMPALPABLE   U. Magic spell; enchantment
___ 22. SINEWY   V. Light can't get through it
___ 23. EFFIGY   W. To invent without preparation
___ 24. IMPERVIOUS   X. Obscured; blocked from view
___ 25. ASSIMILATING   Y. Unfriendly; hostile

Lord of the Flies Vocabulary Matching 2 Answer Key

B - 1. PALL	A.	Thick underbrush providing cover
N - 2. BASTION	B.	A gloomy effect
P - 3. INCREDULITY	C.	Relating to motherhood
T - 4. HIATUS	D.	Made hand motions
G - 5. CYNICISM	E.	Scorn or ridicule
Y - 6. INIMICAL	F.	Scornful
O - 7. SPECIOUS	G.	Attitude scornful of the motives or virtues of others
S - 8. PURGED	H.	Ponderously clumsy
H - 9. ELEPHANTINE	I.	Impenetrable
C - 10. MATERNAL	J.	Crackling sound
U - 11. GLAMOUR	K.	Absorbing
F - 12. DERISIVE	L.	Intangible; not perceived by touch
D - 13. GESTICULATED	M.	A likeness or image
E - 14. DERISION	N.	A well-fortified position
I - 15. INSCRUTABLE	O.	Plausible but actually false
V - 16. OPAQUE	P.	Disbelief
J - 17. CREPITATION	Q.	Incapable of being affected
X - 18. ECLIPSED	R.	Lean and muscular
W - 19. IMPROVISATION	S.	Freed from impurities
A - 20. COVERTS	T.	A break
L - 21. IMPALPABLE	U.	Magic spell; enchantment
R - 22. SINEWY	V.	Light can't get through it
M - 23. EFFIGY	W.	To invent without preparation
Q - 24. IMPERVIOUS	X.	Obscured; blocked from view
K - 25. ASSIMILATING	Y.	Unfriendly; hostile

Copyrighted

Lord of the Flies Vocabulary Matching 3

___ 1. INSCRUTABLE   A. Scornful
___ 2. EXCRUCIATINGLY   B. Tall, pointed formations
___ 3. OBTUSENESS   C. Decorated
___ 4. SKEWED   D. Ponderously clumsy
___ 5. TACITLY   E. Absorbing
___ 6. FESTOONED   F. Impenetrable
___ 7. CYNICISM   G. Intensely painfully
___ 8. INCANTATION   H. Intangible; not perceived by touch
___ 9. EFFIGY   I. Turned to one side
___10. MATERNAL   J. Obscured; blocked from view
___11. ECLIPSED   K. Made hand motions
___12. SANCTITY   L. To criticize or reprimand
___13. GESTICULATED   M. Without being spoken
___14. IMPALPABLE   N. A likeness or image
___15. MYOPIA   O. Thick underbrush providing cover
___16. GLAMOUR   P. A well-fortified position
___17. DERISIVE   Q. Relating to motherhood
___18. PURGED   R. A visual defect like nearsightedness
___19. COVERTS   S. Sacredness; godliness
___20. IMPROVISATION   T. A verbal charm or spell
___21. ELEPHANTINE   U. To invent without preparation
___22. ASSIMILATING   V. Attitude scornful of the motives or virtues of others
___23. PINNACLES   W. Freed from impurities
___24. BASTION   X. Magic spell; enchantment
___25. REBUKE   Y. Dullness; flatness; lack of sharp edges

Lord of the Flies Vocabulary Matching 3 Answer Key

F - 1. INSCRUTABLE	A.	Scornful
G - 2. EXCRUCIATINGLY	B.	Tall, pointed formations
Y - 3. OBTUSENESS	C.	Decorated
I - 4. SKEWED	D.	Ponderously clumsy
M - 5. TACITLY	E.	Absorbing
C - 6. FESTOONED	F.	Impenetrable
V - 7. CYNICISM	G.	Intensely painfully
T - 8. INCANTATION	H.	Intangible; not perceived by touch
N - 9. EFFIGY	I.	Turned to one side
Q - 10. MATERNAL	J.	Obscured; blocked from view
J - 11. ECLIPSED	K.	Made hand motions
S - 12. SANCTITY	L.	To criticize or reprimand
K - 13. GESTICULATED	M.	Without being spoken
H - 14. IMPALPABLE	N.	A likeness or image
R - 15. MYOPIA	O.	Thick underbrush providing cover
X - 16. GLAMOUR	P.	A well-fortified position
A - 17. DERISIVE	Q.	Relating to motherhood
W - 18. PURGED	R.	A visual defect like nearsightedness
O - 19. COVERTS	S.	Sacredness; godliness
U - 20. IMPROVISATION	T.	A verbal charm or spell
D - 21. ELEPHANTINE	U.	To invent without preparation
E - 22. ASSIMILATING	V.	Attitude scornful of the motives or virtues of others
B - 23. PINNACLES	W.	Freed from impurities
P - 24. BASTION	X.	Magic spell; enchantment
L - 25. REBUKE	Y.	Dullness; flatness; lack of sharp edges

Lord of the Flies Vocabulary Matching 4

___ 1. PINNACLES   A. Intensely painfully
___ 2. INSCRUTABLE   B. Incapable of being affected
___ 3. TRUCULENTLY   C. The highest point
___ 4. CYNICISM   D. Tall, pointed formations
___ 5. GLAMOUR   E. Lean and muscular
___ 6. SINEWY   F. Turned to one side
___ 7. ECLIPSED   G. Ponderously clumsy
___ 8. HIATUS   H. Scornful
___ 9. IMPERVIOUS   I. Decorated
___10. PALL   J. Crackling sound
___11. ELEPHANTINE   K. Freed from impurities
___12. APEX   L. Disposed to fight
___13. DERISIVE   M. A likeness or image
___14. IMPALPABLE   N. Intangible; not perceived by touch
___15. EFFIGY   O. Unfriendly; hostile
___16. SKEWED   P. To criticize or reprimand
___17. FESTOONED   Q. Obscured; blocked from view
___18. INIMICAL   R. Attitude scornful of the motives or virtues of others
___19. EXCRUCIATINGLY   S. Magic spell; enchantment
___20. REBUKE   T. Relating to motherhood
___21. GESTICULATED   U. A gloomy effect
___22. MATERNAL   V. Light can't get through it
___23. CREPITATION   W. Impenetrable
___24. OPAQUE   X. Made hand motions
___25. PURGED   Y. A break

Lord of the Flies Vocabulary Matching 4 Answer Key

D - 1. PINNACLES		A. Intensely painfully
W - 2. INSCRUTABLE		B. Incapable of being affected
L - 3. TRUCULENTLY		C. The highest point
R - 4. CYNICISM		D. Tall, pointed formations
S - 5. GLAMOUR		E. Lean and muscular
E - 6. SINEWY		F. Turned to one side
Q - 7. ECLIPSED		G. Ponderously clumsy
Y - 8. HIATUS		H. Scornful
B - 9. IMPERVIOUS		I. Decorated
U - 10. PALL		J. Crackling sound
G - 11. ELEPHANTINE		K. Freed from impurities
C - 12. APEX		L. Disposed to fight
H - 13. DERISIVE		M. A likeness or image
N - 14. IMPALPABLE		N. Intangible; not perceived by touch
M - 15. EFFIGY		O. Unfriendly; hostile
F - 16. SKEWED		P. To criticize or reprimand
I - 17. FESTOONED		Q. Obscured; blocked from view
O - 18. INIMICAL		R. Attitude scornful of the motives or virtues of others
A - 19. EXCRUCIATINGLY		S. Magic spell; enchantment
P - 20. REBUKE		T. Relating to motherhood
X - 21. GESTICULATED		U. A gloomy effect
T - 22. MATERNAL		V. Light can't get through it
J - 23. CREPITATION		W. Impenetrable
V - 24. OPAQUE		X. Made hand motions
K - 25. PURGED		Y. A break

Lord of the Flies Vocabulary Magic Squares 1

Match the definition with the vocabulary word. Put your answers in the magic squares below. When your answers are correct, all columns and rows will add to the same number.

A. OPAQUE
B. REBUKE
C. PALL
D. INSCRUTABLE
E. EFFIGY
F. BASTION
G. SANCTITY
H. TRUCULENTLY
I. PURGED
J. PINNACLES
K. INCREDULITY
L. SPECIOUS
M. MATERNAL
N. TAUT
O. ECLIPSED
P. EBULLIENCE

1. Relating to motherhood
2. A well-fortified position
3. Disposed to fight
4. Obscured; blocked from view
5. Plausible but actually false
6. A gloomy effect
7. Light can't get through it
8. Tall, pointed formations
9. Disbelief
10. Impenetrable
11. To criticize or reprimand
12. Freed from impurities
13. Tight
14. A likeness or image
15. Sacredness; godliness
16. Zestful enthusiasm

A= 7	B= 11	C= 6	D= 10
E= 14	F= 2	G= 15	H= 3
I= 12	J= 8	K= 9	L= 5
M= 1	N= 13	O= 4	P= 16

Lord of the Flies Vocabulary Magic Squares 1 Answer Key

Match the definition with the vocabulary word. Put your answers in the magic squares below. When your answers are correct, all columns and rows will add to the same number.

A. OPAQUE
B. REBUKE
C. PALL
D. INSCRUTABLE
E. EFFIGY
F. BASTION
G. SANCTITY
H. TRUCULENTLY
I. PURGED
J. PINNACLES
K. INCREDULITY
L. SPECIOUS
M. MATERNAL
N. TAUT
O. ECLIPSED
P. EBULLIENCE

1. Relating to motherhood
2. A well-fortified position
3. Disposed to fight
4. Obscured; blocked from view
5. Plausible but actually false
6. A gloomy effect
7. Light can't get through it
8. Tall, pointed formations
9. Disbelief
10. Impenetrable
11. To criticize or reprimand
12. Freed from impurities
13. Tight
14. A likeness or image
15. Sacredness; godliness
16. Zestful enthusiasm

A=7	B=11	C=6	D=10
E=14	F=2	G=15	H=3
I=12	J=8	K=9	L=5
M=1	N=13	O=4	P=16

Lord of the Flies Vocabulary Magic Squares 2

Match the definition with the vocabulary word. Put your answers in the magic squares below. When your answers are correct, all columns and rows will add to the same number.

A. PURGED
B. INCANTATION
C. PROPITATINGLY
D. REBUKE
E. IMPROVISATION
F. ELEPHANTINE
G. TAUT
H. IMPERVIOUS
I. OPAQUE
J. SKEWED
K. HIATUS
L. ASSIMILATING
M. COVERTS
N. TEMPESTUOUSLY
O. APEX
P. EBULLIENCE

1. Incapable of being affected
2. Freed from impurities
3. A verbal charm or spell
4. Tight
5. Turned to one side
6. The highest point
7. Zestful enthusiasm
8. Light can't get through it
9. A break
10. Like a storm; turbulently
11. Thick underbrush providing cover
12. Absorbing
13. To invent without preparation
14. To criticize or reprimand
15. Appeasingly; trying to please
16. Ponderously clumsy

A=	B=	C=	D=
E=	F=	G=	H=
I=	J=	K=	L=
M=	N=	O=	P=

Lord of the Flies Vocabulary Magic Squares 2 Answer Key

Match the definition with the vocabulary word. Put your answers in the magic squares below. When your answers are correct, all columns and rows will add to the same number.

A. PURGED
B. INCANTATION
C. PROPITATINGLY
D. REBUKE
E. IMPROVISATION
F. ELEPHANTINE
G. TAUT
H. IMPERVIOUS
I. OPAQUE
J. SKEWED
K. HIATUS
L. ASSIMILATING
M. COVERTS
N. TEMPESTUOUSLY
O. APEX
P. EBULLIENCE

1. Incapable of being affected
2. Freed from impurities
3. A verbal charm or spell
4. Tight
5. Turned to one side
6. The highest point
7. Zestful enthusiasm
8. Light can't get through it
9. A break
10. Like a storm; turbulently
11. Thick underbrush providing cover
12. Absorbing
13. To invent without preparation
14. To criticize or reprimand
15. Appeasingly; trying to please
16. Ponderously clumsy

A=2	B=3	C=15	D=14
E=13	F=16	G=4	H=1
I=8	J=5	K=9	L=12
M=11	N=10	O=6	P=7

Lord of the Flies Vocabulary Magic Squares 3

Match the definition with the vocabulary word. Put your answers in the magic squares below. When your answers are correct, all columns and rows will add to the same number.

A. PALL
B. GESTICULATED
C. MATERNAL
D. OPAQUE
E. MYOPIA
F. SKEWED

G. BASTION
H. PURGED
I. APEX
J. REBUKE
K. SANCTITY
L. TRUCULENTLY

M. INSCRUTABLE
N. PROPITATINGLY
O. EFFIGY
P. TEMPESTUOUSLY

1. Turned to one side
2. The highest point
3. A likeness or image
4. Light can't get through it
5. Impenetrable
6. Made hand motions
7. Freed from impurities
8. Sacredness; godliness

9. Relating to motherhood
10. Like a storm; turbulently
11. To criticize or reprimand
12. A visual defect like nearsightedness
13. Disposed to fight
14. A well-fortified position
15. A gloomy effect
16. Appeasingly; trying to please

A=	B=	C=	D=
E=	F=	G=	H=
I=	J=	K=	L=
M=	N=	O=	P=

Lord of the Flies Vocabulary Magic Squares 3 Answer Key

Match the definition with the vocabulary word. Put your answers in the magic squares below. When your answers are correct, all columns and rows will add to the same number.

A. PALL
B. GESTICULATED
C. MATERNAL
D. OPAQUE
E. MYOPIA
F. SKEWED
G. BASTION
H. PURGED
I. APEX
J. REBUKE
K. SANCTITY
L. TRUCULENTLY
M. INSCRUTABLE
N. PROPITATINGLY
O. EFFIGY
P. TEMPESTUOUSLY

1. Turned to one side
2. The highest point
3. A likeness or image
4. Light can't get through it
5. Impenetrable
6. Made hand motions
7. Freed from impurities
8. Sacredness; godliness
9. Relating to motherhood
10. Like a storm; turbulently
11. To criticize or reprimand
12. A visual defect like nearsightedness
13. Disposed to fight
14. A well-fortified position
15. A gloomy effect
16. Appeasingly; trying to please

A=15	B=6	C=9	D=4
E=12	F=1	G=14	H=7
I=2	J=11	K=8	L=13
M=5	N=16	O=3	P=10

Lord of the Flies Vocabulary Magic Squares 4

Match the definition with the vocabulary word. Put your answers in the magic squares below. When your answers are correct, all columns and rows will add to the same number.

A. ASSIMILATING
B. CYNICISM
C. INIMICAL
D. PINNACLES
E. MATERNAL
F. INCANTATION
G. EXCRUCIATINGLY
H. IMPALPABLE
I. FESTOONED
J. CREPITATION
K. MYOPIA
L. DECLIVITIES
M. DERISIVE
N. EFFIGY
O. TRUCULENTLY
P. INCREDULITY

1. Unfriendly; hostile
2. Crackling sound
3. A verbal charm or spell
4. Disposed to fight
5. Disbelief
6. Relating to motherhood
7. Decorated
8. Tall, pointed formations
9. Scornful
10. Intangible; not perceived by touch
11. Downward slopes
12. Absorbing
13. Attitude scornful of the motives or virtues of others
14. A visual defect like nearsightedness
15. Intensely painfully
16. A likeness or image

A=	B=	C=	D=
E=	F=	G=	H=
I=	J=	K=	L=
M=	N=	O=	P=

Lord of the Flies Vocabulary Magic Squares 4 Answer Key

Match the definition with the vocabulary word. Put your answers in the magic squares below. When your answers are correct, all columns and rows will add to the same number.

A. ASSIMILATING
B. CYNICISM
C. INIMICAL
D. PINNACLES
E. MATERNAL
F. INCANTATION
G. EXCRUCIATINGLY
H. IMPALPABLE
I. FESTOONED
J. CREPITATION
K. MYOPIA
L. DECLIVITIES
M. DERISIVE
N. EFFIGY
O. TRUCULENTLY
P. INCREDULITY

1. Unfriendly; hostile
2. Crackling sound
3. A verbal charm or spell
4. Disposed to fight
5. Disbelief
6. Relating to motherhood
7. Decorated
8. Tall, pointed formations
9. Scornful
10. Intangible; not perceived by touch
11. Downward slopes
12. Absorbing
13. Attitude scornful of the motives or virtues of others
14. A visual defect like nearsightedness
15. Intensely painfully
16. A likeness or image

A=12	B=13	C=1	D=8
E=6	F=3	G=15	H=10
I=7	J=2	K=14	L=11
M=9	N=16	O=4	P=5

Lord of the Flies Vocabulary Word Search 1

Words are placed backwards, forward, diagonally, up and down. Clues listed below can help you find the words. Circle the hidden vocabulary words in the maze.

```
S D E R I S I V E F N L O W A C O V E R T S Y
I S C I I P G H N K D U B F I P T J X N Y R Y
N C H M M E N T S V C X T F N X E Q C J L G P
E K Y P P C I N Y L P U U I S Z M X R B G D B
W W T E R I T J L N S R S N C R P Q U T N C K
Y R I R O O A K T F D I E C R N E E C C I X Y
D Q L V V U L F I E N A N A U M S L I V T L L
E R U I I S I G C V Y N E N T A B A C A T H
T V D O S R M L A N K C S T A T U A T F T S Y
A N E U A D I A T G O E S S A B E O P I E I N
L X R S T V S M D Z P L Q T L R U L N S P N Y
U G C M I Y S O T D A C E I E N S A G T O C N
C P N T O V A U E P Q K I O E A L P L O R T G
I Y I Z N J T R U C U L E N T L Y M Y O P I A
T E W N J J I J R B E R I F I J R I W N Z T N
S R B M N S N V E Y W T G T F M C Q F E C Y F
E H R U I A J R Z G N E W E A I I X J D X J M
G R I O L B C T B A O C Y Q D U G C Y G D Q M
S W N A D L P L H T I L C R V T T Y A E J K X
R H Q V T K I P E S T I Y K Z P T S W L Q P B
D Y T F R U E E L S S P Q C M V P E N J M F V
Y T K K G L S L N W A S M N S D K K D Q L K Q
C R B M E V A X M C B E L H M S I C I N Y C Z
Z Y G R T P M V M M E D C R E P I T A T I O N
```

A break (6)
A gloomy effect (4)
A likeness or image (6)
A verbal charm or spell (11)
A visual defect like nearsightedness (6)
A well-fortified position (7)
Absorbing (12)
Appeasingly; trying to please (13)
Attitude scornful of the motives or virtues of others (8)
Crackling sound (11)
Decorated (9)
Disbelief (11)
Disposed to fight (11)
Downward slopes (11)
Dullness; flatness; lack of sharp edges (10)
Freed from impurities (6)
Having rich or profuse growth (10)
Impenetrable (11)
Incapable of being affected (10)
Intangible; not perceived by touch (10)
Intensely painfully (14)

Lean and muscular (6)
Light can't get through it (6)
Like a storm; turbulently (13)
Made hand motions (12)
Magic spell; enchantment (7)
Obscured; blocked from view (8)
Plausible but actually false (8)
Ponderously clumsy (11)
Relating to motherhood (8)
Sacredness; godliness (8)
Scorn or ridicule (8)
Scornful (8)
Tall, pointed formations (9)
The highest point (4)
Thick underbrush providing cover (7)
Tight (4)
To criticize or reprimand (6)
To invent without preparation (13)
Turned to one side (6)
Unfriendly; hostile (8)
Without being spoken (7)
Zestful enthusiasm (10)

Lord of the Flies Vocabulary Word Search 1 Answer Key

Words are placed backwards, forward, diagonally, up and down. Clues listed below can help you find the words. Circle the hidden vocabulary words in the maze.

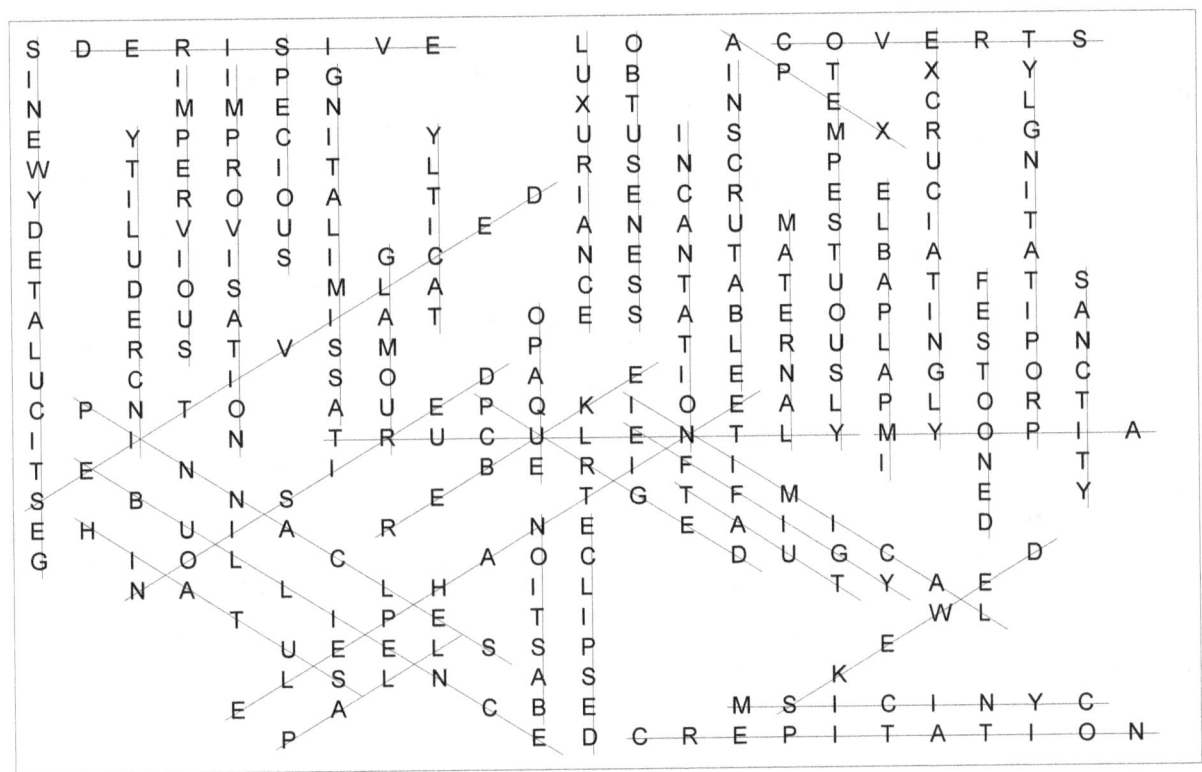

A break (6)
A gloomy effect (4)
A likeness or image (6)
A verbal charm or spell (11)
A visual defect like nearsightedness (6)
A well-fortified position (7)
Absorbing (12)
Appeasingly; trying to please (13)
Attitude scornful of the motives or virtues of others (8)
Crackling sound (11)
Decorated (9)
Disbelief (11)
Disposed to fight (11)
Downward slopes (11)
Dullness; flatness; lack of sharp edges (10)
Freed from impurities (6)
Having rich or profuse growth (10)
Impenetrable (11)
Incapable of being affected (10)
Intangible; not perceived by touch (10)
Intensely painfully (14)

Lean and muscular (6)
Light can't get through it (6)
Like a storm; turbulently (13)
Made hand motions (12)
Magic spell; enchantment (7)
Obscured; blocked from view (8)
Plausible but actually false (8)
Ponderously clumsy (11)
Relating to motherhood (8)
Sacredness; godliness (8)
Scorn or ridicule (8)
Scornful (8)
Tall, pointed formations (9)
The highest point (4)
Thick underbrush providing cover (7)
Tight (4)
To criticize or reprimand (6)
To invent without preparation (13)
Turned to one side (6)
Unfriendly; hostile (8)
Without being spoken (7)
Zestful enthusiasm (10)

Lord of the Flies Vocabulary Word Search 2

Words are placed backwards, forward, diagonally, up and down. Clues listed below can help you find the words. Circle the hidden vocabulary words in the maze.

```
P J Y G D E T A L U C I T S E G X Q R K H J S
R N D R G M Y L D C F M F H M H W Q P Z D E F
O P C K M K A N C K F P T N S N T N F B E C V
P T D M Q C G G N I T A L I M I S S A J C L R
I S R R I J L M P M M L M O P Z Y H J L I Z
T N P M M F A P P N V P S Q P J V I M I P P
A Q I L M T M H H O T A F A B J A Y A D V S F
T N N P E H O V B I B B E Z L Y Y Q T C I E T
I N C R E D U L I T Y L T N E L U C U R T D G
N Q N E G Q R Y S S B E Y H G S L T S E I E Q
G A C B L C P Q S A P Q L N L U U A F P E F X
L I O U M Y F L T B T D I X S O X C E I S F X
Y M V K W N T U Q U E T E U I U U I S T E I Q
I P E E M I R C A G A P O S N T R T T A L G D
N E R P G C W T R I A I S K E S I L O T E Y T
C R T W S I S U C D C Q F E W E A Y O I P P S
A V S N F S P U M E C T C W Y P N T N O H I K
N I I X X M R G P Y R M S E V M C I E N A N D
T O K P J C C S Q R O H K D D E E T D K N N D
A U Q Y X X Q P M Y P P W F Y T L C K N T A H
T S G E G T S E B U L L I E N C E N J G I C Y
I P R Z B R J L H C X Y J A W Y V A Z Z N L D
O D E R I S I O N O B T U S E N E S S N E E V
N O I T A S I V O R P M I D E R I S I V E S J
```

A break (6)
A gloomy effect (4)
A likeness or image (6)
A verbal charm or spell (11)
A visual defect like nearsightedness (6)
A well-fortified position (7)
Absorbing (12)
Appeasingly; trying to please (13)
Attitude scornful of the motives or virtues of others (8)
Crackling sound (11)
Decorated (9)
Disbelief (11)
Disposed to fight (11)
Downward slopes (11)
Dullness; flatness; lack of sharp edges (10)
Freed from impurities (6)
Having rich or profuse growth (10)
Impenetrable (11)
Incapable of being affected (10)
Intangible; not perceived by touch (10)
Intensely painfully (14)

Lean and muscular (6)
Light can't get through it (6)
Like a storm; turbulently (13)
Made hand motions (12)
Magic spell; enchantment (7)
Obscured; blocked from view (8)
Plausible but actually false (8)
Ponderously clumsy (11)
Relating to motherhood (8)
Sacredness; godliness (8)
Scorn or ridicule (8)
Scornful (8)
Tall, pointed formations (9)
The highest point (4)
Thick underbrush providing cover (7)
Tight (4)
To criticize or reprimand (6)
To invent without preparation (13)
Turned to one side (6)
Unfriendly; hostile (8)
Without being spoken (7)
Zestful enthusiasm (10)

Lord of the Flies Vocabulary Word Search 2 Answer Key

Words are placed backwards, forward, diagonally, up and down. Clues listed below can help you find the words. Circle the hidden vocabulary words in the maze.

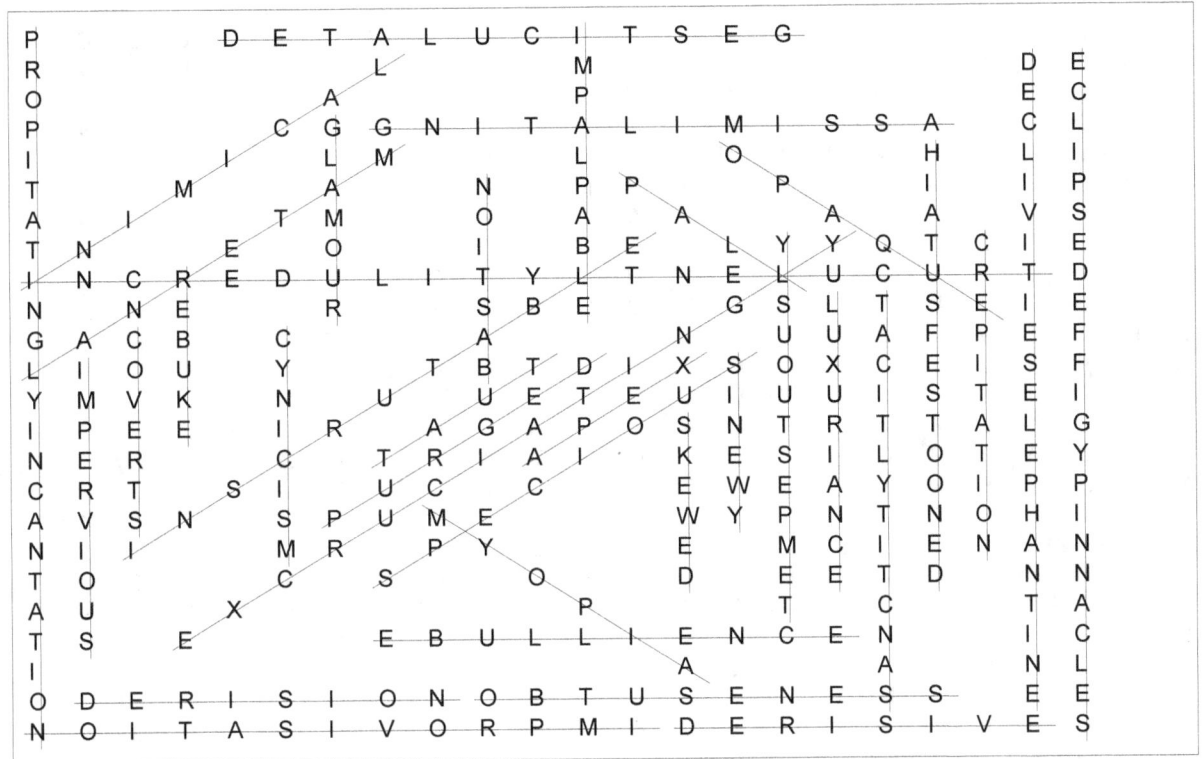

A break (6)
A gloomy effect (4)
A likeness or image (6)
A verbal charm or spell (11)
A visual defect like nearsightedness (6)
A well-fortified position (7)
Absorbing (12)
Appeasingly; trying to please (13)
Attitude scornful of the motives or virtues of others (8)
Crackling sound (11)
Decorated (9)
Disbelief (11)
Disposed to fight (11)
Downward slopes (11)
Dullness; flatness; lack of sharp edges (10)
Freed from impurities (6)
Having rich or profuse growth (10)
Impenetrable (11)
Incapable of being affected (10)
Intangible; not perceived by touch (10)
Intensely painfully (14)

Lean and muscular (6)
Light can't get through it (6)
Like a storm; turbulently (13)
Made hand motions (12)
Magic spell; enchantment (7)
Obscured; blocked from view (8)
Plausible but actually false (8)
Ponderously clumsy (11)
Relating to motherhood (8)
Sacredness; godliness (8)
Scorn or ridicule (8)
Scornful (8)
Tall, pointed formations (9)
The highest point (4)
Thick underbrush providing cover (7)
Tight (4)
To criticize or reprimand (6)
To invent without preparation (13)
Turned to one side (6)
Unfriendly; hostile (8)
Without being spoken (7)
Zestful enthusiasm (10)

Lord of the Flies Vocabulary Word Search 3

Words are placed backwards, forward, diagonally, up and down. Words listed below are included in the maze. Circle the hidden vocabulary words in the maze.

```
E C L I P S E D S R E B U K E K W A H R G E Q
D C I T M S J U G N Z N S C L T I Y U T V S V
E V L M N P O P I Y T H N D R P L O A I J K X
C K D X P I E T I X V A Q U O G M C S T P E M
L Y L J C A N R Z N I Y C Y N A C I S E W W P
I R N E S A L V V R N U M I L H R C I M F E M
V H P I H R V P U I L A T G T E G C M P J D B
I S G P C T F X A E O A C Y D L C Y I E I Z D
T Q E C Q I U Z N B I U Q L D D Y T L S M Q K
I L S R J L S T N C L D S G E Y D J A T P J H
E K T E V M L M U Z S E H N Z S M M T U R P D
S B I P J Y R R N B E H T I E H D F I O O V H
S F C I X R C C V W C Q B T L D B B N U V K H
Q K U T J X W C R H N T N A B N E G G S I B G
W P L A E B Q K P Z E O P T A T X R Z L S A K
M W A T F N J H B P I Q V I T I P L I Y A S V
A C T I F E D I K T L G R P U E N J N S T T K
T O E O R H S A A F L T T O R Y F I G B I I L
E V D N T M Y T I L U D E R C N I F M F O O N
R E R Y P P N U O A B G H P S N Q D I I N N N
N R G K S A N S T O E T B B N A B B K G C F L
A T S R C J X M M Z N V J R I T P N W J Y A W
L S A N C T I T Y P B E U Q A P O E P A L L L
Y S I N E W Y P U R G E D Y H H K S X H C S K
```

APEX	FESTOONED	OPAQUE
ASSIMILATING	GESTICULATED	PALL
BASTION	GLAMOUR	PINNACLES
COVERTS	HIATUS	PROPITATINGLY
CREPITATION	IMPALPABLE	PURGED
CYNICISM	IMPERVIOUS	REBUKE
DECLIVITIES	IMPROVISATION	SANCTITY
DERISION	INCANTATION	SINEWY
DERISIVE	INCREDULITY	SKEWED
EBULLIENCE	INIMICAL	SPECIOUS
ECLIPSED	INSCRUTABLE	TACITLY
EFFIGY	LUXURIANCE	TAUT
ELEPHANTINE	MATERNAL	TEMPESTUOUSLY
EXCRUCIATINGLY	MYOPIA	TRUCULENTLY

Lord of the Flies Vocabulary Word Search 3 Answer Key

Words are placed backwards, forward, diagonally, up and down. Words listed below are included in the maze. Circle the hidden vocabulary words in the maze.

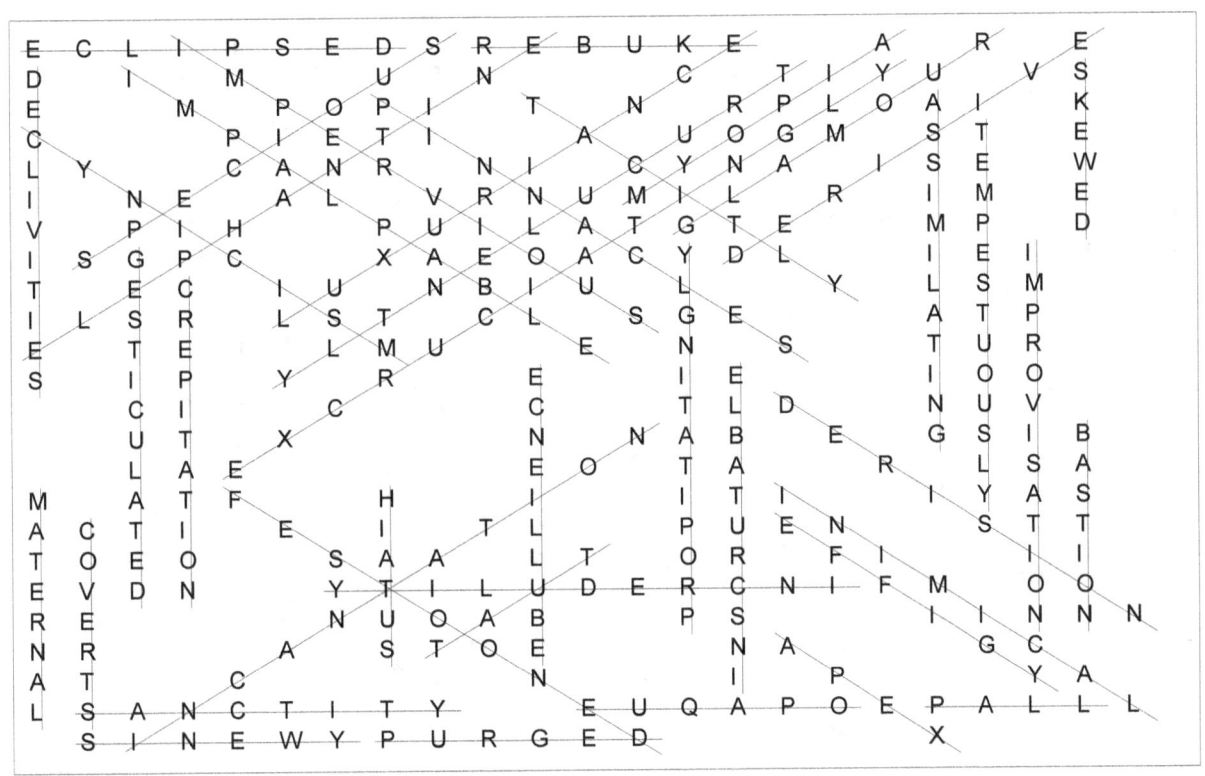

APEX	FESTOONED	OPAQUE
ASSIMILATING	GESTICULATED	PALL
BASTION	GLAMOUR	PINNACLES
COVERTS	HIATUS	PROPITATINGLY
CREPITATION	IMPALPABLE	PURGED
CYNICISM	IMPERVIOUS	REBUKE
DECLIVITIES	IMPROVISATION	SANCTITY
DERISION	INCANTATION	SINEWY
DERISIVE	INCREDULITY	SKEWED
EBULLIENCE	INIMICAL	SPECIOUS
ECLIPSED	INSCRUTABLE	TACITLY
EFFIGY	LUXURIANCE	TAUT
ELEPHANTINE	MATERNAL	TEMPESTUOUSLY
EXCRUCIATINGLY	MYOPIA	TRUCULENTLY

Lord of the Flies Vocabulary Word Search 4

Words are placed backwards, forward, diagonally, up and down. Words listed below are included in the maze. Circle the hidden vocabulary words in the maze.

```
I N I M I C A L I N C A N T A T I O N T D G K
L P P X H Q H Z I M P R O V I S A T I O N V H
K Q S O G B B N D B Q B K Y M X R M L L Q T B
K T E J B H L Z Y A X X K T R N D X A R C E M
P E L B A T U R C S N I J I Z T E N B F W M W
V L C T J X U C N T G J Y T V L R J P I W P D
Q H A R A R V S G I S L G C S E I H A N M E E
G J N G J U C S E O G T T N T H S S L C G S X
Z R N F E S T O O N E D S A H G I J L R M T C
M Y I S K R J C I O E E M S C N V A U E K U R
E Y P Z E H L T M I I S T F E I E P T D S O U
N N O V M Q A X T T M B S W F T T E Q U X U C
I M O P Q T L Z I A Q P Y Q E A C L W L S S I
T C H L I G B V P T Y H E K V L M R Y I E L A
N X E P A A I S D I X C U R I I G L G T U Y T
A B O F L L Q E D P M B Z P V M K L Y Y Q C I
H R B S C N W Q E E E P S H Z I Y L A T A W N
P E W E P E F X R R L E A Z T S O X J M P T G
E F D W K E J D I C D C G L W S H U N Y O Y L
L F L S G Z C Y S Q R Q Y S P A S B S X C U Y
E I H P G M H I I L D X E C N A I R U X U L R
V G W P R D S D O Y Q Z W Z H D B C N N P L H
L Y F K T W D L N U G E S T I C U L A T E D D
C Y N I C I S M Q V S C T R U C U L E N T L Y
```

APEX	GESTICULATED	OPAQUE
ASSIMILATING	GLAMOUR	PALL
BASTION	HIATUS	PINNACLES
COVERTS	IMPALPABLE	PROPITATINGLY
CREPITATION	IMPERVIOUS	PURGED
CYNICISM	IMPROVISATION	REBUKE
DECLIVITIES	INCANTATION	SANCTITY
DERISION	INCREDULITY	SINEWY
DERISIVE	INIMICAL	SKEWED
ECLIPSED	INSCRUTABLE	SPECIOUS
EFFIGY	LUXURIANCE	TACITLY
ELEPHANTINE	MATERNAL	TAUT
EXCRUCIATINGLY	MYOPIA	TEMPESTUOUSLY
FESTOONED	OBTUSENESS	TRUCULENTLY

Lord of the Flies Vocabulary Word Search 4 Answer Key

Words are placed backwards, forward, diagonally, up and down. Words listed below are included in the maze. Circle the hidden vocabulary words in the maze.

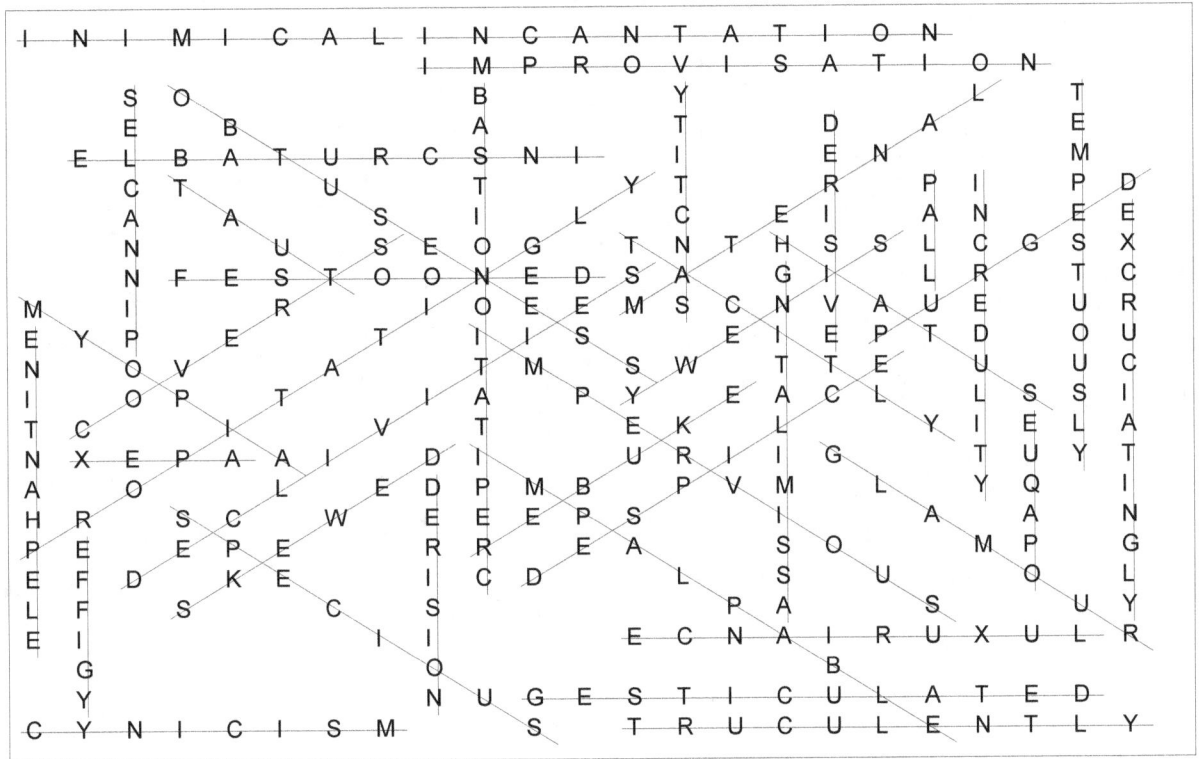

APEX	GESTICULATED	OPAQUE
ASSIMILATING	GLAMOUR	PALL
BASTION	HIATUS	PINNACLES
COVERTS	IMPALPABLE	PROPITATINGLY
CREPITATION	IMPERVIOUS	PURGED
CYNICISM	IMPROVISATION	REBUKE
DECLIVITIES	INCANTATION	SANCTITY
DERISION	INCREDULITY	SINEWY
DERISIVE	INIMICAL	SKEWED
ECLIPSED	INSCRUTABLE	SPECIOUS
EFFIGY	LUXURIANCE	TACITLY
ELEPHANTINE	MATERNAL	TAUT
EXCRUCIATINGLY	MYOPIA	TEMPESTUOUSLY
FESTOONED	OBTUSENESS	TRUCULENTLY

Lord of the Flies Vocabulary Crossword 1

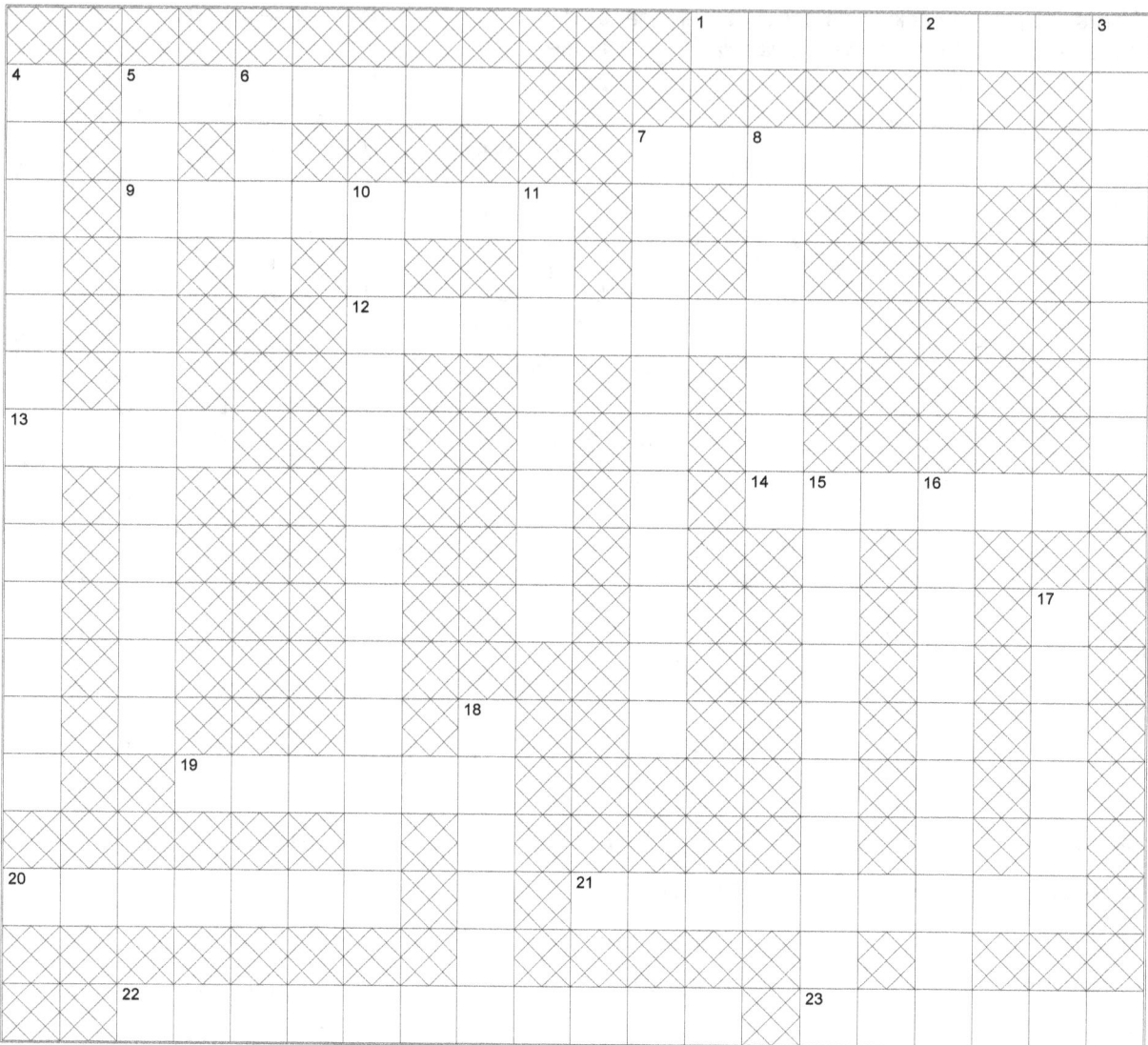

Across
1. Obscured; blocked from view
5. Magic spell; enchantment
7. Without being spoken
9. Plausible but actually false
12. Tall, pointed formations
13. Tight
14. Lean and muscular
19. A likeness or image
20. A well-fortified position
21. Decorated
22. A verbal charm or spell
23. Turned to one side

Down
2. A gloomy effect
3. Scorn or ridicule
4. Like a storm; turbulently
5. Made hand motions
6. The highest point
7. Disposed to fight
8. Thick underbrush providing cover
10. To invent without preparation
11. Sacredness; godliness
15. Incapable of being affected
16. Zestful enthusiasm
17. Freed from impurities
18. A visual defect like nearsightedness

Lord of the Flies Vocabulary Crossword 1 Answer Key

Across
1. Obscured; blocked from view
5. Magic spell; enchantment
7. Without being spoken
9. Plausible but actually false
12. Tall, pointed formations
13. Tight
14. Lean and muscular
19. A likeness or image
20. A well-fortified position
21. Decorated
22. A verbal charm or spell
23. Turned to one side

Down
2. A gloomy effect
3. Scorn or ridicule
4. Like a storm; turbulently
5. Made hand motions
6. The highest point
7. Disposed to fight
8. Thick underbrush providing cover
10. To invent without preparation
11. Sacredness; godliness
15. Incapable of being affected
16. Zestful enthusiasm
17. Freed from impurities
18. A visual defect like nearsightedness

Lord of the Flies Vocabulary Crossword 2

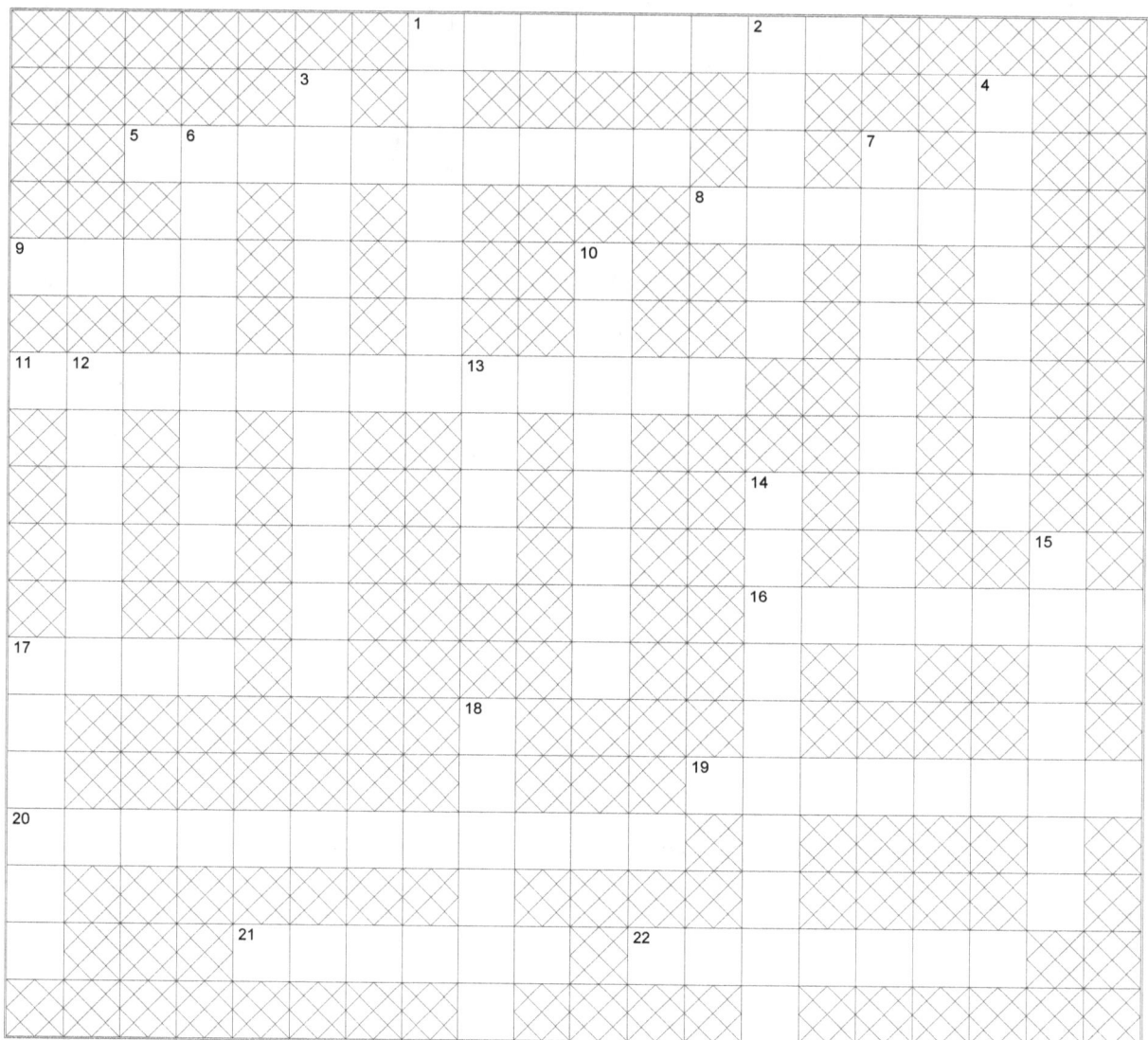

Across
1. Attitude scornful of the motives or virtues of others
5. Incapable of being affected
8. To criticize or reprimand
9. Tight
11. To invent without preparation
16. Without being spoken
17. A gloomy effect
19. Scorn or ridicule
20. Made hand motions
21. Light can't get through it
22. A well-fortified position

Down
1. Thick underbrush providing cover
2. Lean and muscular
3. Downward slopes
4. Plausible but actually false
6. Relating to motherhood
7. Having rich or profuse growth
10. Unfriendly; hostile
12. A visual defect like nearsightedness
13. The highest point
14. Dullness; flatness; lack of sharp edges
15. Magic spell; enchantment
17. Freed from impurities
18. A break

Lord of the Flies Vocabulary Crossword 2 Answer Key

							1 C	Y	N	I	C	I	2 S	M					
					3 D		O						I				4 S		
		5 I	6 M	P	E	R	V	I	O	U	S		N		7 L		P		
			A		C		E					8 R	E	B	U	K	E		
9 T	A	U	T		L		R			10 I			W		X		C		
			E		I		T			N			Y		U		I		
11 I	12 M	P	R	O	V	I	S	13 A	T	I	O	N			R		O		
	Y		N		I			P		M					I		U		
	O		A		T			E		I			14 O		A		S		
	P		L		I			X		C			B		N			15 G	
	I				E					A			16 T	A	C	I	T	L	Y
17 P	A	L	L		S					L			U		E			A	
U								18 H					S					M	
R								I				19 D	E	R	I	S	I	O	N
20 G	E	S	T	I	C	U	L	A	T	E	D		N					U	
E								T					E					R	
D				21 O	P	A	Q	U	E		22 B	A	S	T	I	O	N		
								S					S						

Across
1. Attitude scornful of the motives or virtues of others
5. Incapable of being affected
8. To criticize or reprimand
9. Tight
11. To invent without preparation
16. Without being spoken
17. A gloomy effect
19. Scorn or ridicule
20. Made hand motions
21. Light can't get through it
22. A well-fortified position

.

Down
1. Thick underbrush providing cover
2. Lean and muscular
3. Downward slopes
4. Plausible but actually false
6. Relating to motherhood
7. Having rich or profuse growth
10. Unfriendly; hostile
12. A visual defect like nearsightedness
13. The highest point
14. Dullness; flatness; lack of sharp edges
15. Magic spell; enchantment
17. Freed from impurities
18. A break

Lord of the Flies Vocabulary Crossword 3

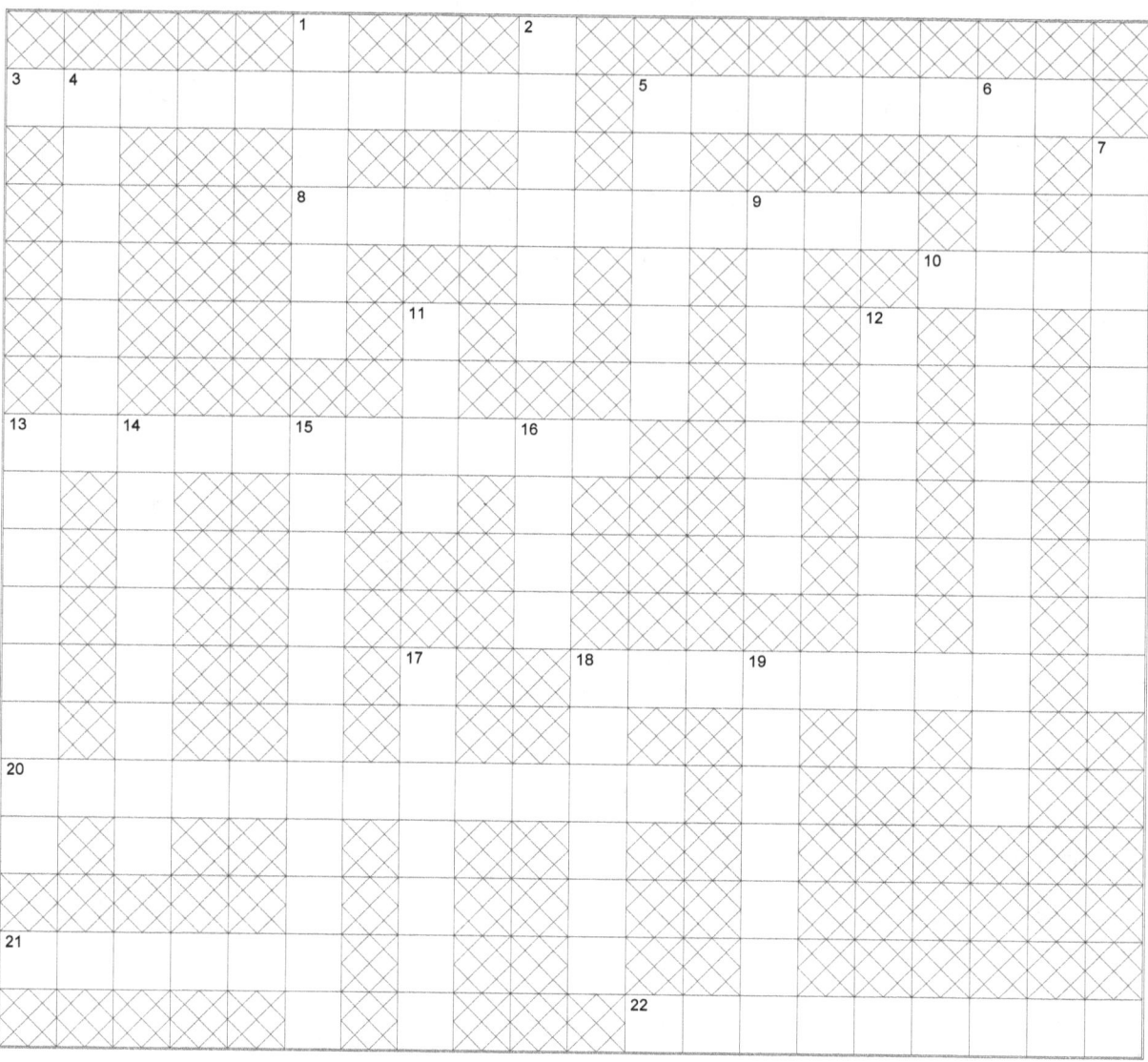

Across
3. Zestful enthusiasm
5. Sacredness; godliness
8. Disposed to fight
10. The highest point
13. Disbelief
18. Plausible but actually false
20. Absorbing
21. Light can't get through it
22. Decorated

Down
1. A break
2. To criticize or reprimand
4. A well-fortified position
5. Turned to one side
6. Like a storm; turbulently
7. Having rich or profuse growth
9. Without being spoken
11. A gloomy effect
12. Scorn or ridicule
13. Unfriendly; hostile
14. Attitude scornful of the motives or virtues of others
15. Downward slopes
16. Tight
17. Magic spell; enchantment
18. Lean and muscular
19. Thick underbrush providing cover

Lord of the Flies Vocabulary Crossword 3 Answer Key

Across
- 3. Zestful enthusiasm
- 5. Sacredness; godliness
- 8. Disposed to fight
- 10. The highest point
- 13. Disbelief
- 18. Plausible but actually false
- 20. Absorbing
- 21. Light can't get through it
- 22. Decorated

Down
- 1. A break
- 2. To criticize or reprimand
- 4. A well-fortified position
- 5. Turned to one side
- 6. Like a storm; turbulently
- 7. Having rich or profuse growth
- 9. Without being spoken
- 11. A gloomy effect
- 12. Scorn or ridicule
- 13. Unfriendly; hostile
- 14. Attitude scornful of the motives or virtues of others
- 15. Downward slopes
- 16. Tight
- 17. Magic spell; enchantment
- 18. Lean and muscular
- 19. Thick underbrush providing cover

Solution Grid

Across answers:
- 3. EBULLIENCE
- 5. SANCTITY
- 8. TRUCULENT
- 10. APEX
- 13. INCREDULITY
- 18. SPECIOUS
- 20. ASSIMILATING
- 21. OPAQUE
- 22. FESTOONED

Down answers:
- 1. HIATUS
- 2. REBUKE
- 4. BASTION
- 5. SKEWED
- 6. TEMPESTUOUSLY
- 7. LUXURIANT
- 9. TACITLY
- 11. PALL
- 12. DERISION
- 13. INIMICAL
- 14. CYNICISM
- 15. DECLIVITIES
- 16. TAUT
- 17. GLAMOURS
- 18. SINEWY
- 19. COVERT

Lord of the Flies Vocabulary Crossword 4

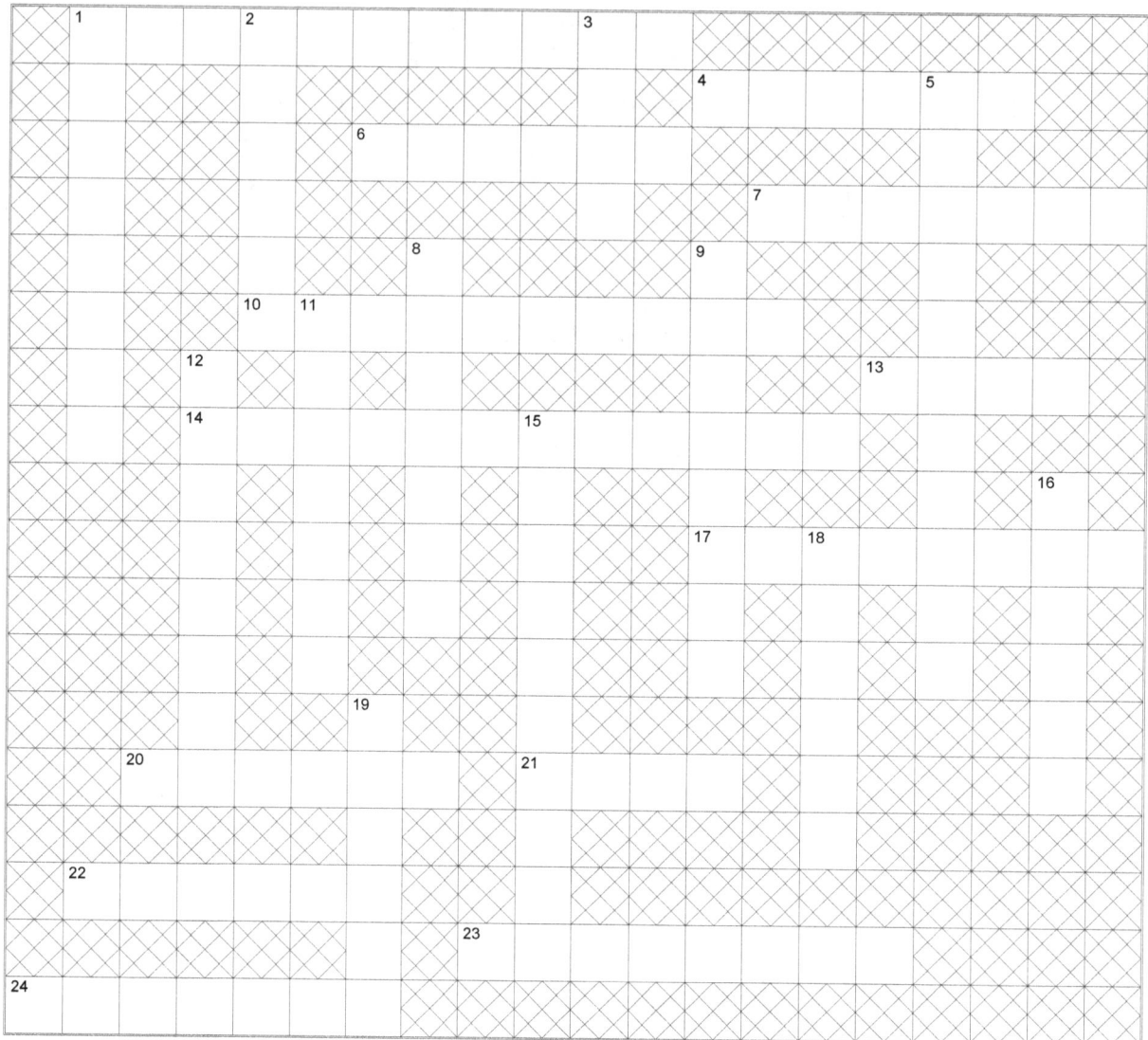

Across
1. Disbelief
4. Turned to one side
6. A break
7. Thick underbrush providing cover
10. Zestful enthusiasm
13. A gloomy effect
14. Absorbing
17. Plausible but actually false
20. A visual defect like nearsightedness
21. The highest point
22. Light can't get through it
23. Scorn or ridicule
24. Without being spoken

Down
1. Unfriendly; hostile
2. To criticize or reprimand
3. Tight
5. Ponderously clumsy
8. Magic spell; enchantment
9. Obscured; blocked from view
11. A well-fortified position
12. Sacredness; godliness
15. Having rich or profuse growth
16. Freed from impurities
18. A likeness or image
19. Lean and muscular

Lord of the Flies Vocabulary Crossword 4 Answer Key

	1 I	N	2 C	R	E	D	U	L	I	3 T	Y					
	N		E							A		4 S	K	E	5 W	E	D
	I		B			6 H	I	A	T	U	S				E	
	M		U							T		7 C	O	V	E	R	T	S
	I		K			8 G						9 E			P	
	C	10 E	11 B	U	L	L	I	E	N	C	E			13 P	H	
	A		12 S		A		A				L			P	A	L	L
	L	14 A	S	S	I	M	15 I	L	A	T	I	N	G		N	
		N		T		O		U			P			T		16 P
		C		I		U		X		17 S	18 P	E	C	I	O	U	S
		T		O		R		U		E		F		N		R
		I		N				R		D		F		E		G
		T			19 S			I				I				E
		20 M	Y	O	P	I	A		21 A	P	E	X		G		D
					N				N					Y	
	22 O	P	A	Q	U	E		23 C						
					W			D	E	R	I	S	I	O	N
24 T	A	C	I	T	L	Y

Across
1. Disbelief
4. Turned to one side
6. A break
7. Thick underbrush providing cover
10. Zestful enthusiasm
13. A gloomy effect
14. Absorbing
17. Plausible but actually false
20. A visual defect like nearsightedness
21. The highest point
22. Light can't get through it
23. Scorn or ridicule
24. Without being spoken

Down
1. Unfriendly; hostile
2. To criticize or reprimand
3. Tight
5. Ponderously clumsy
8. Magic spell; enchantment
9. Obscured; blocked from view
11. A well-fortified position
12. Sacredness; godliness
15. Having rich or profuse growth
16. Freed from impurities
18. A likeness or image
19. Lean and muscular

Lord of the Flies Vocabulary Juggle Letters 1

1. SNLNAIECP = 1. _____
   Tall, pointed formations

2. AILTPENNEHE = 2. _____
   Ponderously clumsy

3. YFIGFE = 3. _____
   A likeness or image

4. APOEUQ = 4. _____
   Light can't get through it

5. EUCLUXNAIR = 5. _____
   Having rich or profuse growth

6. UOBSSNESET = 6. _____
   Dullness; flatness; lack of sharp edges

7. BIRANEUTCLS = 7. _____
   Impenetrable

8. TAITANNONCI = 8. _____
   A verbal charm or spell

9. ITCYTSAN = 9. _____
   Sacredness; godliness

10. TSONABI =10. _____
    A well-fortified position

11. ENIYSW =11. _____
    Lean and muscular

12. CAITLYT =12. _____
    Without being spoken

13. IAYOMP =13. _____
    A visual defect like nearsightedness

14. ILSPEECD =14. _____
    Obscured; blocked from view

15. ECVSITLDIIE =15. _____
    Downward slopes

Lord of the Flies Vocabulary Juggle Letters 1 Answer Key

1. SNLNAIECP = 1. PINNACLES
Tall, pointed formations

2. AILTPENNEHE = 2. ELEPHANTINE
Ponderously clumsy

3. YFIGFE = 3. EFFIGY
A likeness or image

4. APOEUQ = 4. OPAQUE
Light can't get through it

5. EUCLUXNAIR = 5. LUXURIANCE
Having rich or profuse growth

6. UOBSSNESET = 6. OBTUSENESS
Dullness; flatness; lack of sharp edges

7. BIRANEUTCLS = 7. INSCRUTABLE
Impenetrable

8. TAITANNONCI = 8. INCANTATION
A verbal charm or spell

9. ITCYTSAN = 9. SANCTITY
Sacredness; godliness

10. TSONABI =10. BASTION
A well-fortified position

11. ENIYSW =11. SINEWY
Lean and muscular

12. CAITLYT =12. TACITLY
Without being spoken

13. IAYOMP =13. MYOPIA
A visual defect like nearsightedness

14. ILSPEECD =14. ECLIPSED
Obscured; blocked from view

15. ECVSITLDIIE =15. DECLIVITIES
Downward slopes

Copyrighted

Lord of the Flies Vocabulary Juggle Letters 2

1. EGPRUD = 1. _____
   Freed from impurities

2. DOOETNSEF = 2. _____
   Decorated

3. TNAIINACOTN = 3. _____
   A verbal charm or spell

4. SGLTECEADIUT = 4. _____
   Made hand motions

5. EEIUCLENLB = 5. _____
   Zestful enthusiasm

6. CIUSSOPE = 6. _____
   Plausible but actually false

7. MUOGLAR = 7. _____
   Magic spell; enchantment

8. EUKEBR = 8. _____
   To criticize or reprimand

9. OSNDRIIE = 9. _____
   Scorn or ridicule

10. AEMANTRL = 10. _____
    Relating to motherhood

11. CINAIILM = 11. _____
    Unfriendly; hostile

12. PTIOOVARIISNM = 12. _____
    To invent without preparation

13. YPOMIA = 13. _____
    A visual defect like nearsightedness

14. LGOPYRNTPTIAI = 14. _____
    Appeasingly; trying to please

15. LPLA = 15. _____
    A gloomy effect

Lord of the Flies Vocabulary Juggle Letters 2 Answer Key

1. EGPURD = 1. PURGED
   Freed from impurities

2. DOOETNSEF = 2. FESTOONED
   Decorated

3. TNAIINACOTN = 3. INCANTATION
   A verbal charm or spell

4. SGLTECEADIUT = 4. GESTICULATED
   Made hand motions

5. EEIUCLENLB = 5. EBULLIENCE
   Zestful enthusiasm

6. CIUSSOPE = 6. SPECIOUS
   Plausible but actually false

7. MUOGLAR = 7. GLAMOUR
   Magic spell; enchantment

8. EUKEBR = 8. REBUKE
   To criticize or reprimand

9. OSNDRIIE = 9. DERISION
   Scorn or ridicule

10. AEMANTRL =10. MATERNAL
    Relating to motherhood

11. CINAIILM =11. INIMICAL
    Unfriendly; hostile

12. PTIOOVARIISNM =12. IMPROVISATION
    To invent without preparation

13. YPOMIA =13. MYOPIA
    A visual defect like nearsightedness

14. LGOPYRNTPTIAI =14. PROPITATINGLY
    Appeasingly; trying to please

15. LPLA =15. PALL
    A gloomy effect

Lord of the Flies Vocabulary Juggle Letters 3

1. IILCMAIN = 1. _____
   Unfriendly; hostile

2. ITLTCAY = 2. _____
   Without being spoken

3. TDICERULYNI = 3. _____
   Disbelief

4. UTAT = 4. _____
   Tight

5. ESBSTSENOU = 5. _____
   Dullness; flatness; lack of sharp edges

6. XAREUICTIGNCLY = 6. _____
   Intensely painfully

7. AOPEQU = 7. _____
   Light can't get through it

8. RALMTEAN = 8. _____
   Relating to motherhood

9. NISCIMCY = 9. _____
   Attitude scornful of the motives or virtues of others

10. ERTCOSV = 10. _____
    Thick underbrush providing cover

11. EIGDSTCAUELT = 11. _____
    Made hand motions

12. ORICNPTATIE = 12. _____
    Crackling sound

13. TYASTNCI = 13. _____
    Sacredness; godliness

14. REEKBU = 14. _____
    To criticize or reprimand

15. LIBPAMLEPA = 15. _____
    Intangible; not perceived by touch

Lord of the Flies Vocabulary Juggle Letters 3 Answer Key

1. IILCMAIN = 1. INIMICAL
Unfriendly; hostile

2. ITLTCAY = 2. TACITLY
Without being spoken

3. TDICERULYNI = 3. INCREDULITY
Disbelief

4. UTAT = 4. TAUT
Tight

5. ESBSTSENOU = 5. OBTUSENESS
Dullness; flatness; lack of sharp edges

6. XAREUICTIGNCLY = 6. EXCRUCIATINGLY
Intensely painfully

7. AOPEQU = 7. OPAQUE
Light can't get through it

8. RALMTEAN = 8. MATERNAL
Relating to motherhood

9. NISCIMCY = 9. CYNICISM
Attitude scornful of the motives or virtues of others

10. ERTCOSV =10. COVERTS
Thick underbrush providing cover

11. EIGDSTCAUELT =11. GESTICULATED
Made hand motions

12. ORICNPTATIE =12. CREPITATION
Crackling sound

13. TYASTNCI =13. SANCTITY
Sacredness; godliness

14. REEKBU =14. REBUKE
To criticize or reprimand

15. LIBPAMLEPA =15. IMPALPABLE
Intangible; not perceived by touch

Lord of the Flies Vocabulary Juggle Letters 4

1. ICNTPEAOITR = 1. _____
   Crackling sound

2. EUNCBRISLTA = 2. _____
   Impenetrable

3. LEPNCANIS = 3. _____
   Tall, pointed formations

4. EUGDRP = 4. _____
   Freed from impurities

5. LDSCPEEI = 5. _____
   Obscured; blocked from view

6. AHITUS = 6. _____
   A break

7. CIYCSMNI = 7. _____
   Attitude scornful of the motives or virtues of others

8. NSAOTIB = 8. _____
   A well-fortified position

9. ALYTCTI = 9. _____
   Without being spoken

10. MNCILAII = 10. _____
    Unfriendly; hostile

11. CGIDSUETAETL = 11. _____
    Made hand motions

12. VEDIECIITSL = 12. _____
    Downward slopes

13. PAOQEU = 13. _____
    Light can't get through it

14. TYNTRLULUCE = 14. _____
    Disposed to fight

15. LTUEIICXNRCYAG = 15. _____
    Intensely painfully

Lord of the Flies Vocabulary Juggle Letters 4 Answer Key

1. ICNTPEAOITR = 1. CREPITATION
   Crackling sound

2. EUNCBRISLTA = 2. INSCRUTABLE
   Impenetrable

3. LEPNCANIS = 3. PINNACLES
   Tall, pointed formations

4. EUGDRP = 4. PURGED
   Freed from impurities

5. LDSCPEEI = 5. ECLIPSED
   Obscured; blocked from view

6. AHITUS = 6. HIATUS
   A break

7. CIYCSMNI = 7. CYNICISM
   Attitude scornful of the motives or virtues of others

8. NSAOTIB = 8. BASTION
   A well-fortified position

9. ALYTCTI = 9. TACITLY
   Without being spoken

10. MNCILAII = 10. INIMICAL
    Unfriendly; hostile

11. CGIDSUETAETL = 11. GESTICULATED
    Made hand motions

12. VEDIECIITSL = 12. DECLIVITIES
    Downward slopes

13. PAOQEU = 13. OPAQUE
    Light can't get through it

14. TYNTRLULUCE = 14. TRUCULENTLY
    Disposed to fight

15. LTUEIICXNRCYAG = 15. EXCRUCIATINGLY
    Intensely painfully

APEX	The highest point
ASSIMILATING	Absorbing
BASTION	A well-fortified position
COVERTS	Thick underbrush providing cover
CREPITATION	Crackling sound
CYNICISM	Attitude scornful of the motives or virtues of others
DECLIVITIES	Downward slopes

DERISION	Scorn or ridicule
DERISIVE	Scornful
EBULLIENCE	Zestful enthusiasm
ECLIPSED	Obscured; blocked from view
EFFIGY	A likeness or image
ELEPHANTINE	Ponderously clumsy
EXCRUCIATINGLY	Intensely painfully

FESTOONED	Decorated
GESTICULATED	Made hand motions
GLAMOUR	Magic spell; enchantment
HIATUS	A break
IMPALPABLE	Intangible; not perceived by touch
IMPERVIOUS	Incapable of being affected
IMPROVISATION	To invent without preparation

INCANTATION	A verbal charm or spell
INCREDULITY	Disbelief
INIMICAL	Unfriendly; hostile
INSCRUTABLE	Impenetrable
LUXURIANCE	Having rich or profuse growth
MATERNAL	Relating to motherhood
MYOPIA	A visual defect like nearsightedness

OBTUSENESS	Dullness; flatness; lack of sharp edges
OPAQUE	Light can't get through it
PALL	A gloomy effect
PINNACLES	Tall, pointed formations
PROPITATINGLY	Appeasingly; trying to please
PURGED	Freed from impurities
REBUKE	To criticize or reprimand

SANCTITY	Sacredness; godliness
SINEWY	Lean and muscular
SKEWED	Turned to one side
SPECIOUS	Plausible but actually false
TACITLY	Without being spoken
TAUT	Tight
TEMPESTUOUSLY	Like a storm; turbulently

TRUCULENTLY | **Disposed to fight**

Lord of the Flies Vocabulary

TRUCULENTLY	FESTOONED	REBUKE	IMPERVIOUS	INCREDULITY
SANCTITY	OBTUSENESS	LUXURIANCE	ELEPHANTINE	EBULLIENCE
GESTICULATED	DECLIVITIES	FREE SPACE	PINNACLES	INIMICAL
MATERNAL	IMPROVISATION	CREPITATION	COVERTS	IMPALPABLE
MYOPIA	APEX	PURGED	TACITLY	ASSIMILATING

Lord of the Flies Vocabulary

ECLIPSED	BASTION	HIATUS	EFFIGY	SINEWY
GLAMOUR	SKEWED	DERISIVE	CYNICISM	PROPITATINGLY
EXCRUCIATINGLY	SPECIOUS	FREE SPACE	PALL	TEMPESTUOUSLY
DERISION	INSCRUTABLE	OPAQUE	ASSIMILATING	TACITLY
PURGED	APEX	MYOPIA	IMPALPABLE	COVERTS

Lord of the Flies Vocabulary

COVERTS	HIATUS	BASTION	TACITLY	IMPALPABLE
EFFIGY	SPECIOUS	DECLIVITIES	PURGED	INSCRUTABLE
SKEWED	INCANTATION	FREE SPACE	INCREDULITY	EBULLIENCE
LUXURIANCE	OBTUSENESS	CREPITATION	APEX	EXCRUCIATINGLY
ELEPHANTINE	IMPROVISATION	IMPERVIOUS	PROPITATINGLY	FESTOONED

Lord of the Flies Vocabulary

INIMICAL	DERISION	REBUKE	TEMPESTUOUSLY	MATERNAL
PALL	TRUCULENTLY	SANCTITY	PINNACLES	GLAMOUR
CYNICISM	GESTICULATED	FREE SPACE	ASSIMILATING	SINEWY
ECLIPSED	DERISIVE	MYOPIA	FESTOONED	PROPITATINGLY
IMPERVIOUS	IMPROVISATION	ELEPHANTINE	EXCRUCIATINGLY	APEX

Lord of the Flies Vocabulary

REBUKE	CYNICISM	SPECIOUS	INCANTATION	MYOPIA
IMPROVISATION	FESTOONED	DERISIVE	INSCRUTABLE	EFFIGY
ECLIPSED	INCREDULITY	FREE SPACE	EBULLIENCE	SINEWY
TEMPESTUOUSLY	PINNACLES	PURGED	IMPALPABLE	EXCRUCIATINGLY
INIMICAL	LUXURIANCE	OPAQUE	MATERNAL	GESTICULATED

Lord of the Flies Vocabulary

ELEPHANTINE	BASTION	SANCTITY	PROPITATINGLY	APEX
IMPERVIOUS	PALL	CREPITATION	DECLIVITIES	HIATUS
OBTUSENESS	SKEWED	FREE SPACE	TACITLY	GLAMOUR
COVERTS	TRUCULENTLY	DERISION	GESTICULATED	MATERNAL
OPAQUE	LUXURIANCE	INIMICAL	EXCRUCIATINGLY	IMPALPABLE

Lord of the Flies Vocabulary

IMPERVIOUS	IMPALPABLE	SPECIOUS	ELEPHANTINE	FESTOONED
CREPITATION	PROPITATINGLY	GESTICULATED	LUXURIANCE	SKEWED
INSCRUTABLE	INCANTATION	FREE SPACE	HIATUS	SANCTITY
MYOPIA	EFFIGY	PINNACLES	BASTION	ASSIMILATING
TACITLY	EBULLIENCE	PURGED	SINEWY	CYNICISM

Lord of the Flies Vocabulary

DECLIVITIES	DERISION	MATERNAL	OBTUSENESS	ECLIPSED
OPAQUE	TEMPESTUOUSLY	EXCRUCIATINGLY	COVERTS	APEX
PALL	INCREDULITY	FREE SPACE	REBUKE	INIMICAL
GLAMOUR	TRUCULENTLY	TAUT	CYNICISM	SINEWY
PURGED	EBULLIENCE	TACITLY	ASSIMILATING	BASTION

Lord of the Flies Vocabulary

FESTOONED	PINNACLES	MYOPIA	SINEWY	MATERNAL
EBULLIENCE	EFFIGY	ASSIMILATING	DERISION	SKEWED
INSCRUTABLE	BASTION	FREE SPACE	TRUCULENTLY	APEX
REBUKE	IMPERVIOUS	CREPITATION	OPAQUE	SANCTITY
ELEPHANTINE	TACITLY	INIMICAL	HIATUS	EXCRUCIATINGLY

Lord of the Flies Vocabulary

PROPITATINGLY	PURGED	OBTUSENESS	ECLIPSED	INCREDULITY
DECLIVITIES	COVERTS	CYNICISM	IMPROVISATION	PALL
GESTICULATED	TAUT	FREE SPACE	INCANTATION	LUXURIANCE
SPECIOUS	IMPALPABLE	DERISIVE	EXCRUCIATINGLY	HIATUS
INIMICAL	TACITLY	ELEPHANTINE	SANCTITY	OPAQUE

Lord of the Flies Vocabulary

COVERTS	IMPALPABLE	PALL	IMPROVISATION	TEMPESTUOUSLY
DERISION	DERISIVE	INIMICAL	EXCRUCIATINGLY	CREPITATION
SANCTITY	ECLIPSED	FREE SPACE	ELEPHANTINE	HIATUS
REBUKE	GESTICULATED	FESTOONED	PURGED	INCREDULITY
TRUCULENTLY	MYOPIA	EBULLIENCE	IMPERVIOUS	CYNICISM

Lord of the Flies Vocabulary

SINEWY	ASSIMILATING	PROPITATINGLY	GLAMOUR	INSCRUTABLE
EFFIGY	LUXURIANCE	PINNACLES	OBTUSENESS	OPAQUE
TAUT	MATERNAL	FREE SPACE	SKEWED	DECLIVITIES
TACITLY	SPECIOUS	INCANTATION	CYNICISM	IMPERVIOUS
EBULLIENCE	MYOPIA	TRUCULENTLY	INCREDULITY	PURGED

Lord of the Flies Vocabulary

TACITLY	DECLIVITIES	CYNICISM	INIMICAL	DERISIVE
MATERNAL	ELEPHANTINE	PROPITATINGLY	CREPITATION	INCREDULITY
SKEWED	IMPERVIOUS	FREE SPACE	APEX	LUXURIANCE
TAUT	INCANTATION	FESTOONED	IMPALPABLE	EBULLIENCE
MYOPIA	OPAQUE	ASSIMILATING	COVERTS	REBUKE

Lord of the Flies Vocabulary

TEMPESTUOUSLY	GLAMOUR	EFFIGY	TRUCULENTLY	ECLIPSED
SANCTITY	INSCRUTABLE	PURGED	PINNACLES	BASTION
PALL	HIATUS	FREE SPACE	IMPROVISATION	DERISION
OBTUSENESS	EXCRUCIATINGLY	SINEWY	REBUKE	COVERTS
ASSIMILATING	OPAQUE	MYOPIA	EBULLIENCE	IMPALPABLE

Lord of the Flies Vocabulary

DECLIVITIES	PROPITATINGLY	SANCTITY	ELEPHANTINE	MYOPIA
DERISION	EBULLIENCE	PURGED	COVERTS	BASTION
SPECIOUS	IMPALPABLE	FREE SPACE	TRUCULENTLY	CYNICISM
TACITLY	ECLIPSED	IMPROVISATION	OBTUSENESS	HIATUS
REBUKE	TEMPESTUOUSLY	LUXURIANCE	GESTICULATED	PALL

Lord of the Flies Vocabulary

MATERNAL	INSCRUTABLE	CREPITATION	INIMICAL	PINNACLES
INCREDULITY	EXCRUCIATINGLY	SINEWY	IMPERVIOUS	OPAQUE
FESTOONED	ASSIMILATING	FREE SPACE	APEX	TAUT
GLAMOUR	EFFIGY	SKEWED	PALL	GESTICULATED
LUXURIANCE	TEMPESTUOUSLY	REBUKE	HIATUS	OBTUSENESS

Lord of the Flies Vocabulary

BASTION	ELEPHANTINE	TACITLY	SPECIOUS	IMPROVISATION
SKEWED	INIMICAL	IMPERVIOUS	INCREDULITY	APEX
LUXURIANCE	INSCRUTABLE	FREE SPACE	PALL	EBULLIENCE
CYNICISM	HIATUS	DERISION	OPAQUE	OBTUSENESS
DECLIVITIES	SANCTITY	INCANTATION	FESTOONED	PROPITATINGLY

Lord of the Flies Vocabulary

SINEWY	EXCRUCIATINGLY	TRUCULENTLY	EFFIGY	PINNACLES
IMPALPABLE	DERISIVE	CREPITATION	GESTICULATED	TEMPESTUOUSLY
ECLIPSED	GLAMOUR	FREE SPACE	COVERTS	MYOPIA
REBUKE	ASSIMILATING	MATERNAL	PROPITATINGLY	FESTOONED
INCANTATION	SANCTITY	DECLIVITIES	OBTUSENESS	OPAQUE

Lord of the Flies Vocabulary

ASSIMILATING	EBULLIENCE	FESTOONED	MYOPIA	TAUT
INSCRUTABLE	BASTION	LUXURIANCE	OBTUSENESS	MATERNAL
GLAMOUR	PALL	FREE SPACE	COVERTS	SPECIOUS
DECLIVITIES	PURGED	INIMICAL	REBUKE	PROPITATINGLY
CYNICISM	DERISIVE	GESTICULATED	TACITLY	INCANTATION

Lord of the Flies Vocabulary

IMPERVIOUS	APEX	OPAQUE	SKEWED	SANCTITY
IMPROVISATION	CREPITATION	EXCRUCIATINGLY	ELEPHANTINE	INCREDULITY
IMPALPABLE	PINNACLES	FREE SPACE	TEMPESTUOUSLY	ECLIPSED
EFFIGY	DERISION	HIATUS	INCANTATION	TACITLY
GESTICULATED	DERISIVE	CYNICISM	PROPITATINGLY	REBUKE

Lord of the Flies Vocabulary

INIMICAL	INSCRUTABLE	GESTICULATED	MATERNAL	INCREDULITY
CYNICISM	TRUCULENTLY	PURGED	DERISIVE	PINNACLES
LUXURIANCE	EBULLIENCE	FREE SPACE	SPECIOUS	ELEPHANTINE
FESTOONED	ECLIPSED	EXCRUCIATINGLY	IMPROVISATION	COVERTS
TACITLY	TEMPESTUOUSLY	INCANTATION	OPAQUE	PALL

Lord of the Flies Vocabulary

IMPERVIOUS	DECLIVITIES	CREPITATION	EFFIGY	ASSIMILATING
IMPALPABLE	PROPITATINGLY	BASTION	APEX	OBTUSENESS
TAUT	GLAMOUR	FREE SPACE	SKEWED	HIATUS
SINEWY	DERISION	REBUKE	PALL	OPAQUE
INCANTATION	TEMPESTUOUSLY	TACITLY	COVERTS	IMPROVISATION

Lord of the Flies Vocabulary

PINNACLES	CREPITATION	IMPERVIOUS	MATERNAL	SKEWED
DERISION	TEMPESTUOUSLY	ASSIMILATING	MYOPIA	GESTICULATED
INIMICAL	APEX	FREE SPACE	SINEWY	SANCTITY
TAUT	REBUKE	OPAQUE	TRUCULENTLY	INSCRUTABLE
ELEPHANTINE	PROPITATINGLY	PURGED	BASTION	COVERTS

Lord of the Flies Vocabulary

INCANTATION	HIATUS	FESTOONED	TACITLY	SPECIOUS
IMPALPABLE	EXCRUCIATINGLY	INCREDULITY	LUXURIANCE	DECLIVITIES
PALL	OBTUSENESS	FREE SPACE	EBULLIENCE	CYNICISM
GLAMOUR	IMPROVISATION	DERISIVE	COVERTS	BASTION
PURGED	PROPITATINGLY	ELEPHANTINE	INSCRUTABLE	TRUCULENTLY

Lord of the Flies Vocabulary

CYNICISM	INCANTATION	COVERTS	CREPITATION	FESTOONED
IMPALPABLE	INIMICAL	OPAQUE	SANCTITY	TAUT
PINNACLES	DERISIVE	FREE SPACE	SPECIOUS	REBUKE
EBULLIENCE	GLAMOUR	LUXURIANCE	EXCRUCIATINGLY	IMPROVISATION
DERISION	ASSIMILATING	MYOPIA	TACITLY	BASTION

Lord of the Flies Vocabulary

PALL	ELEPHANTINE	GESTICULATED	SINEWY	INCREDULITY
EFFIGY	MATERNAL	PROPITATINGLY	APEX	PURGED
HIATUS	IMPERVIOUS	FREE SPACE	DECLIVITIES	TRUCULENTLY
TEMPESTUOUSLY	OBTUSENESS	INSCRUTABLE	BASTION	TACITLY
MYOPIA	ASSIMILATING	DERISION	IMPROVISATION	EXCRUCIATINGLY

Lord of the Flies Vocabulary

OBTUSENESS	CREPITATION	OPAQUE	SINEWY	EFFIGY
BASTION	INSCRUTABLE	IMPALPABLE	IMPROVISATION	ELEPHANTINE
APEX	PURGED	FREE SPACE	TACITLY	SKEWED
GLAMOUR	DECLIVITIES	INIMICAL	PALL	CYNICISM
SANCTITY	PROPITATINGLY	INCREDULITY	MATERNAL	IMPERVIOUS

Lord of the Flies Vocabulary

SPECIOUS	LUXURIANCE	ECLIPSED	TAUT	GESTICULATED
ASSIMILATING	TEMPESTUOUSLY	COVERTS	INCANTATION	DERISION
MYOPIA	HIATUS	FREE SPACE	TRUCULENTLY	FESTOONED
DERISIVE	REBUKE	EXCRUCIATINGLY	IMPERVIOUS	MATERNAL
INCREDULITY	PROPITATINGLY	SANCTITY	CYNICISM	PALL

Lord of the Flies Vocabulary

TACITLY	PURGED	LUXURIANCE	SINEWY	GLAMOUR
ECLIPSED	MATERNAL	SKEWED	EFFIGY	PALL
INIMICAL	APEX	FREE SPACE	REBUKE	ASSIMILATING
DECLIVITIES	PINNACLES	TAUT	DERISION	GESTICULATED
PROPITATINGLY	OPAQUE	DERISIVE	TEMPESTUOUSLY	COVERTS

Lord of the Flies Vocabulary

ELEPHANTINE	MYOPIA	FESTOONED	IMPALPABLE	CREPITATION
HIATUS	SANCTITY	EXCRUCIATINGLY	IMPROVISATION	BASTION
INCREDULITY	CYNICISM	FREE SPACE	OBTUSENESS	SPECIOUS
EBULLIENCE	INSCRUTABLE	INCANTATION	COVERTS	TEMPESTUOUSLY
DERISIVE	OPAQUE	PROPITATINGLY	GESTICULATED	DERISION

Lord of the Flies Vocabulary

DERISION	APEX	CYNICISM	FESTOONED	MYOPIA
INSCRUTABLE	DERISIVE	REBUKE	ECLIPSED	SANCTITY
SPECIOUS	PALL	FREE SPACE	TACITLY	SKEWED
COVERTS	OBTUSENESS	IMPROVISATION	IMPERVIOUS	LUXURIANCE
EXCRUCIATINGLY	EBULLIENCE	DECLIVITIES	MATERNAL	TAUT

Lord of the Flies Vocabulary

TRUCULENTLY	GESTICULATED	GLAMOUR	INCANTATION	OPAQUE
EFFIGY	PINNACLES	PROPITATINGLY	HIATUS	CREPITATION
ASSIMILATING	BASTION	FREE SPACE	ELEPHANTINE	TEMPESTUOUSLY
INIMICAL	INCREDULITY	SINEWY	TAUT	MATERNAL
DECLIVITIES	EBULLIENCE	EXCRUCIATINGLY	LUXURIANCE	IMPERVIOUS

www.ingramcontent.com/pod-product-compliance
Lightning Source LLC
Chambersburg PA
CBHW081457070526
44586CB00019B/2391